Welcome to the Stylish Anime Characters Coloring Book!

Thank you for choosing this coloring book filled with 33 unique and fashionable anime characters. Each page is designed to spark your creativity and provide a relaxing, enjoyable experience.

Have Fun!

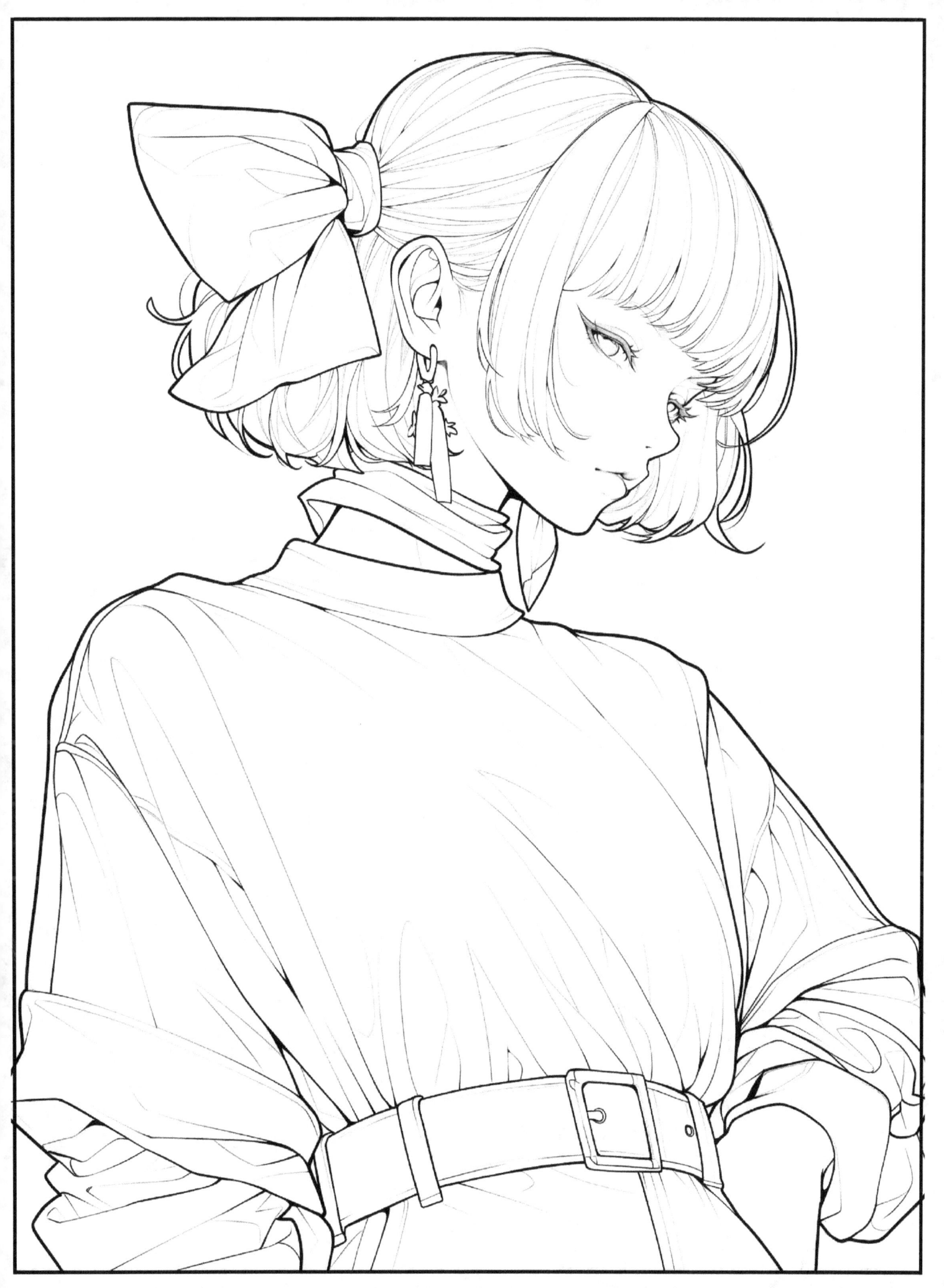

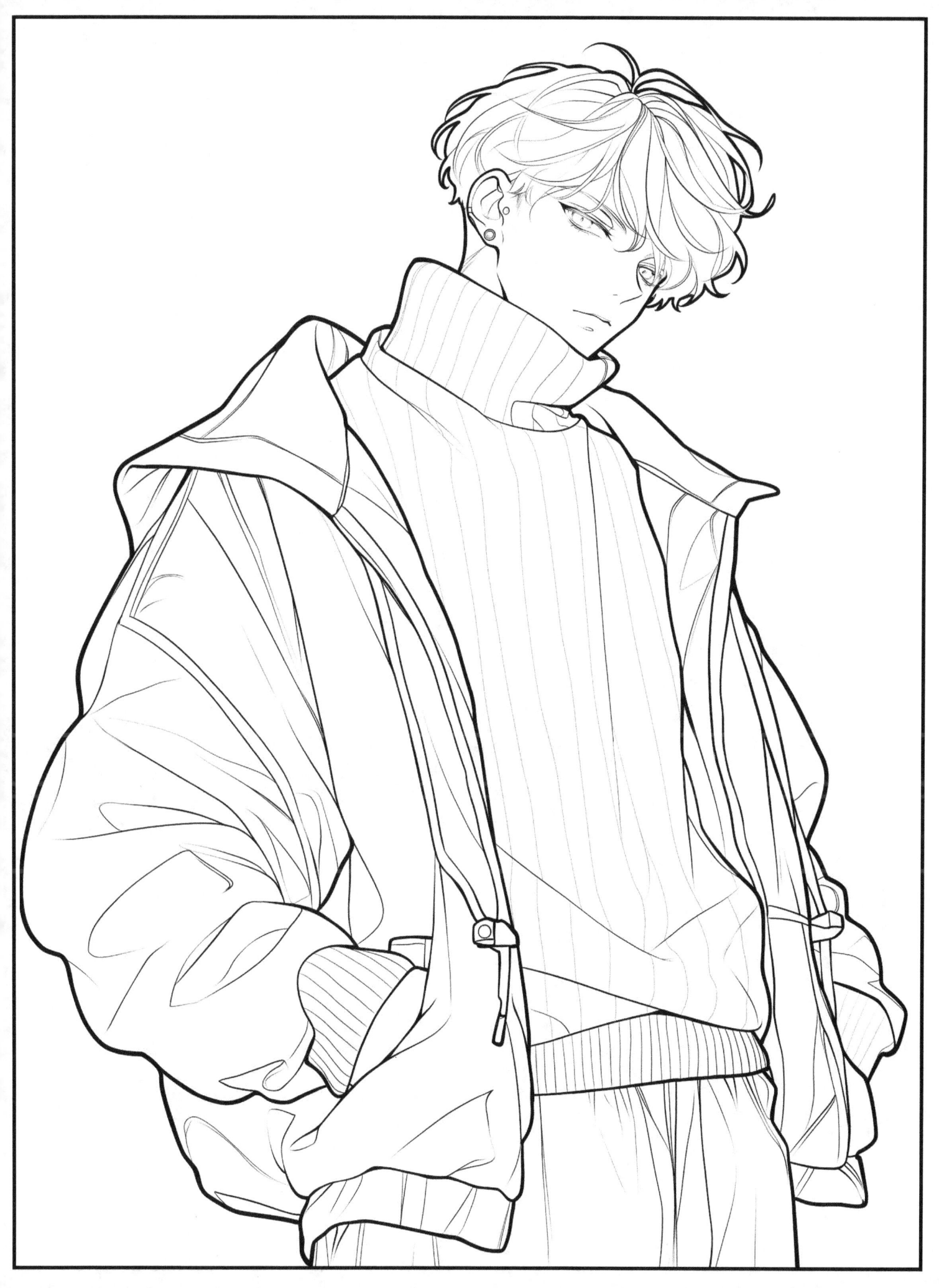

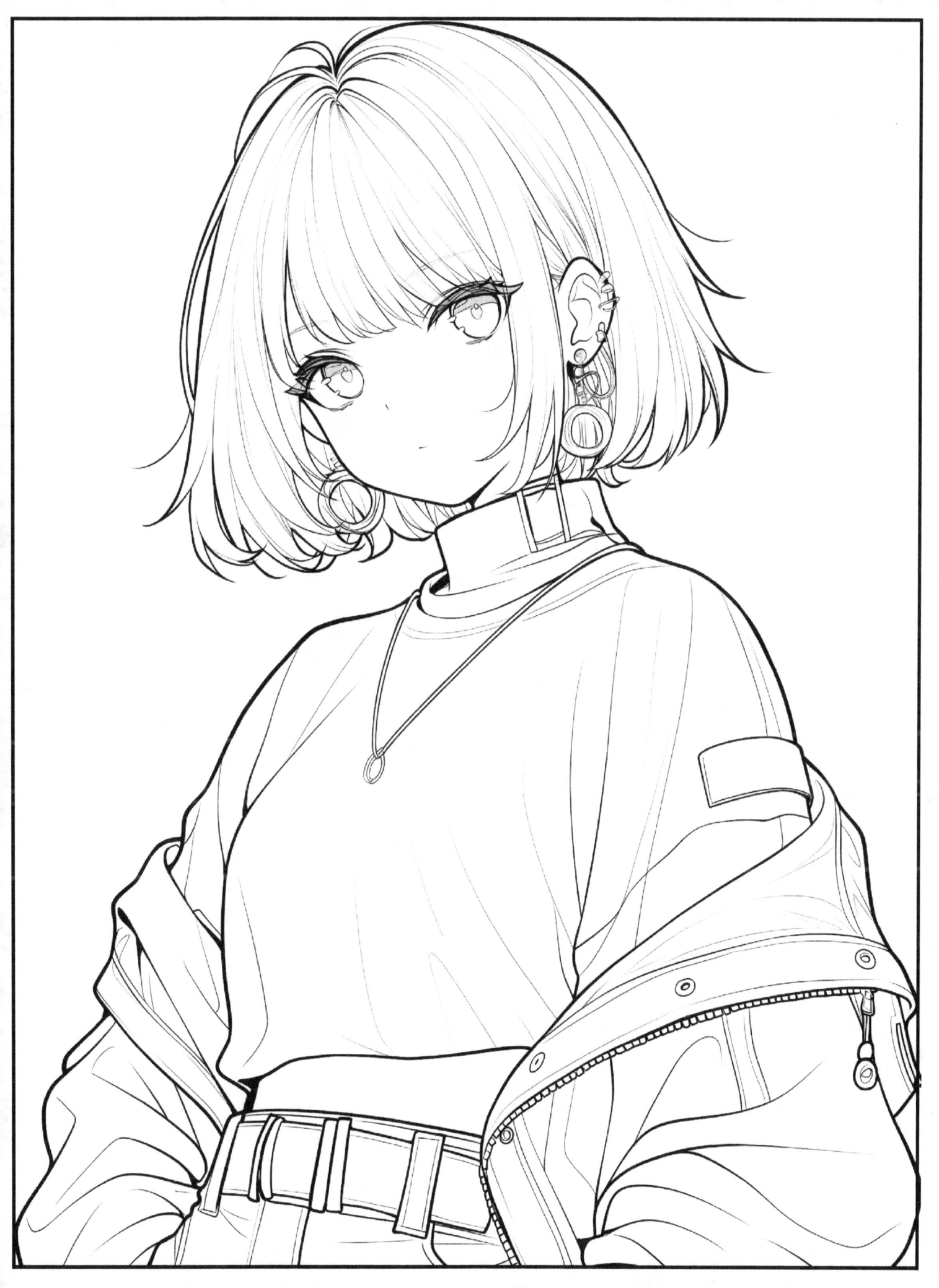

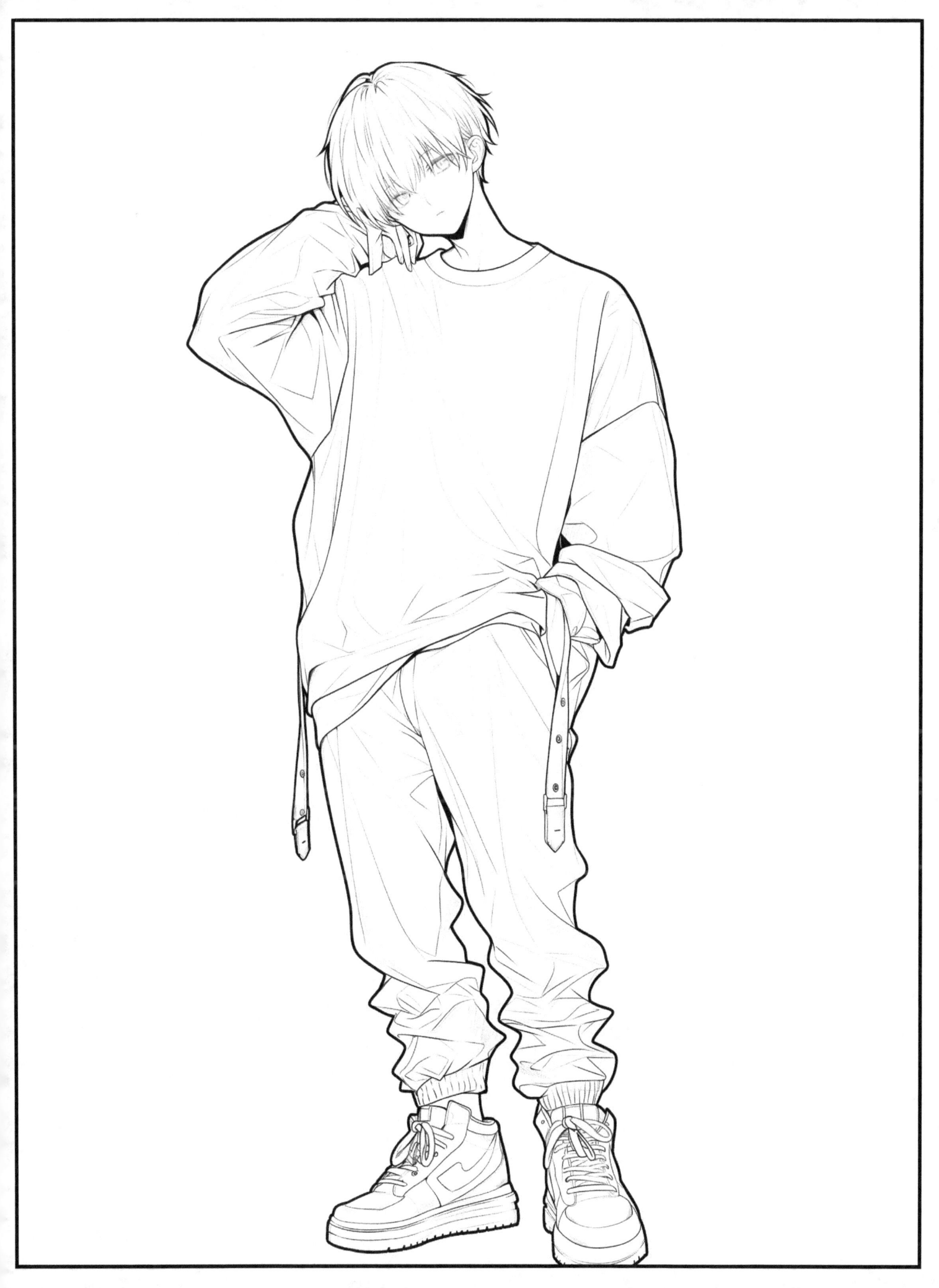

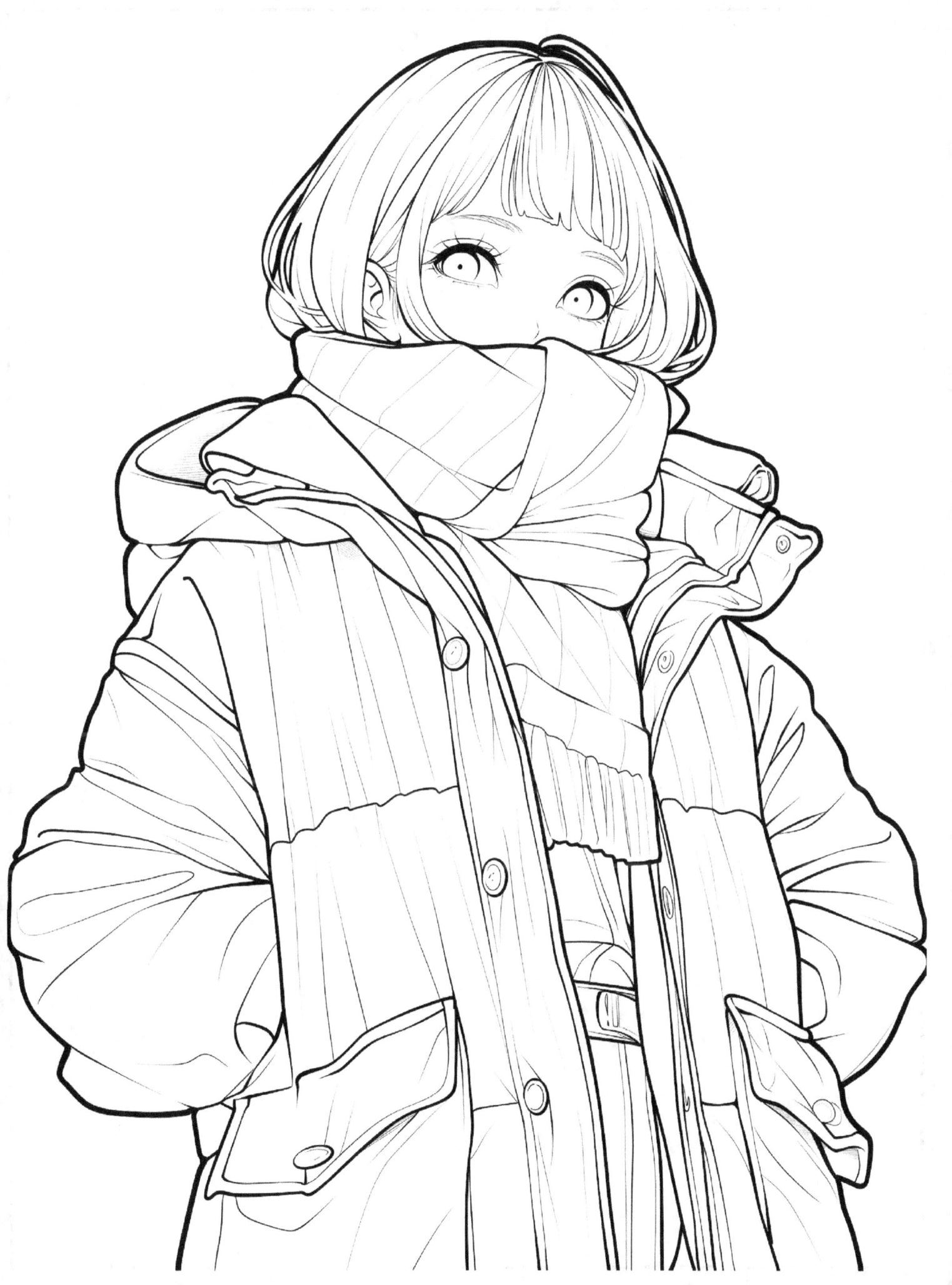

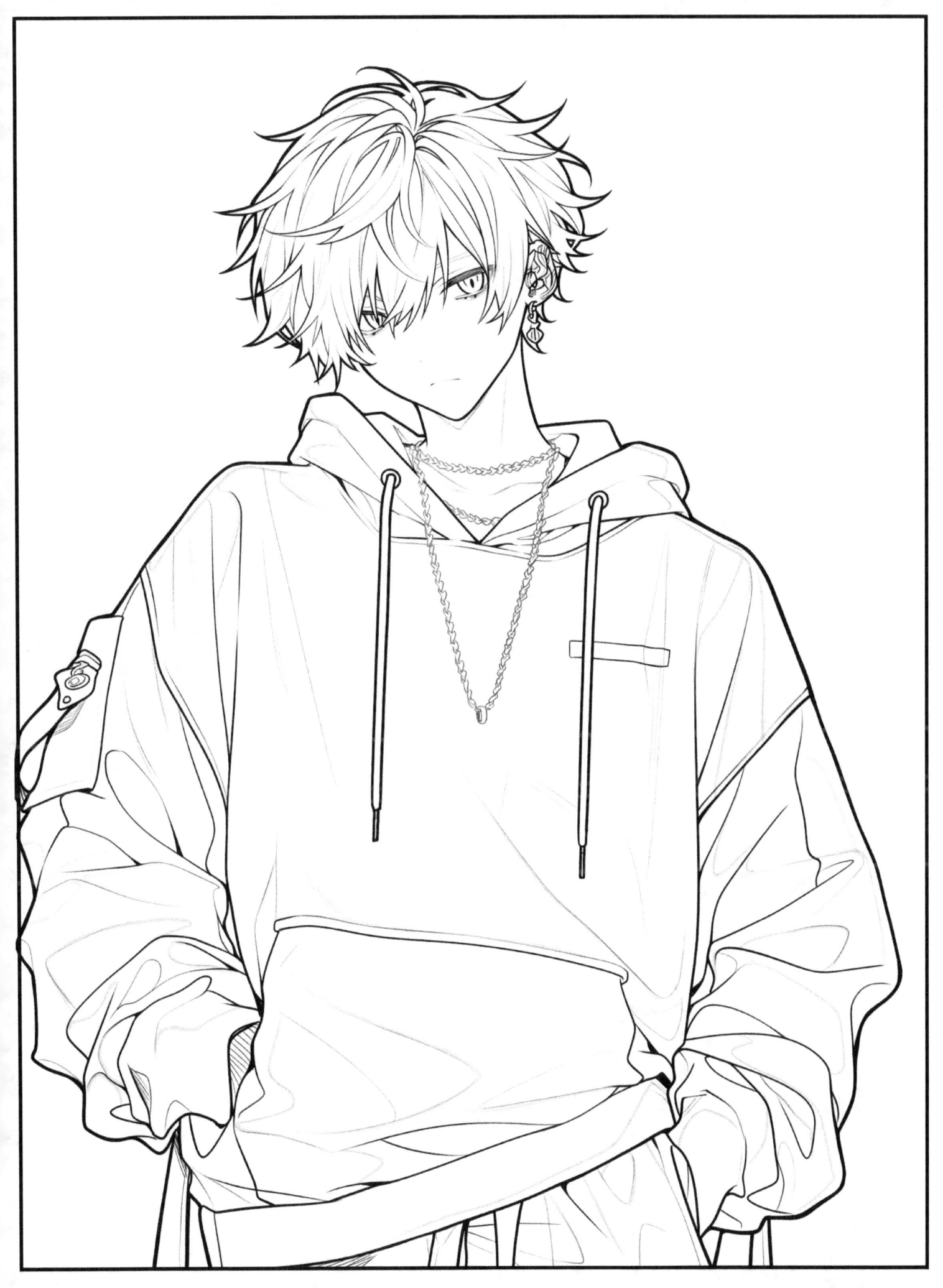

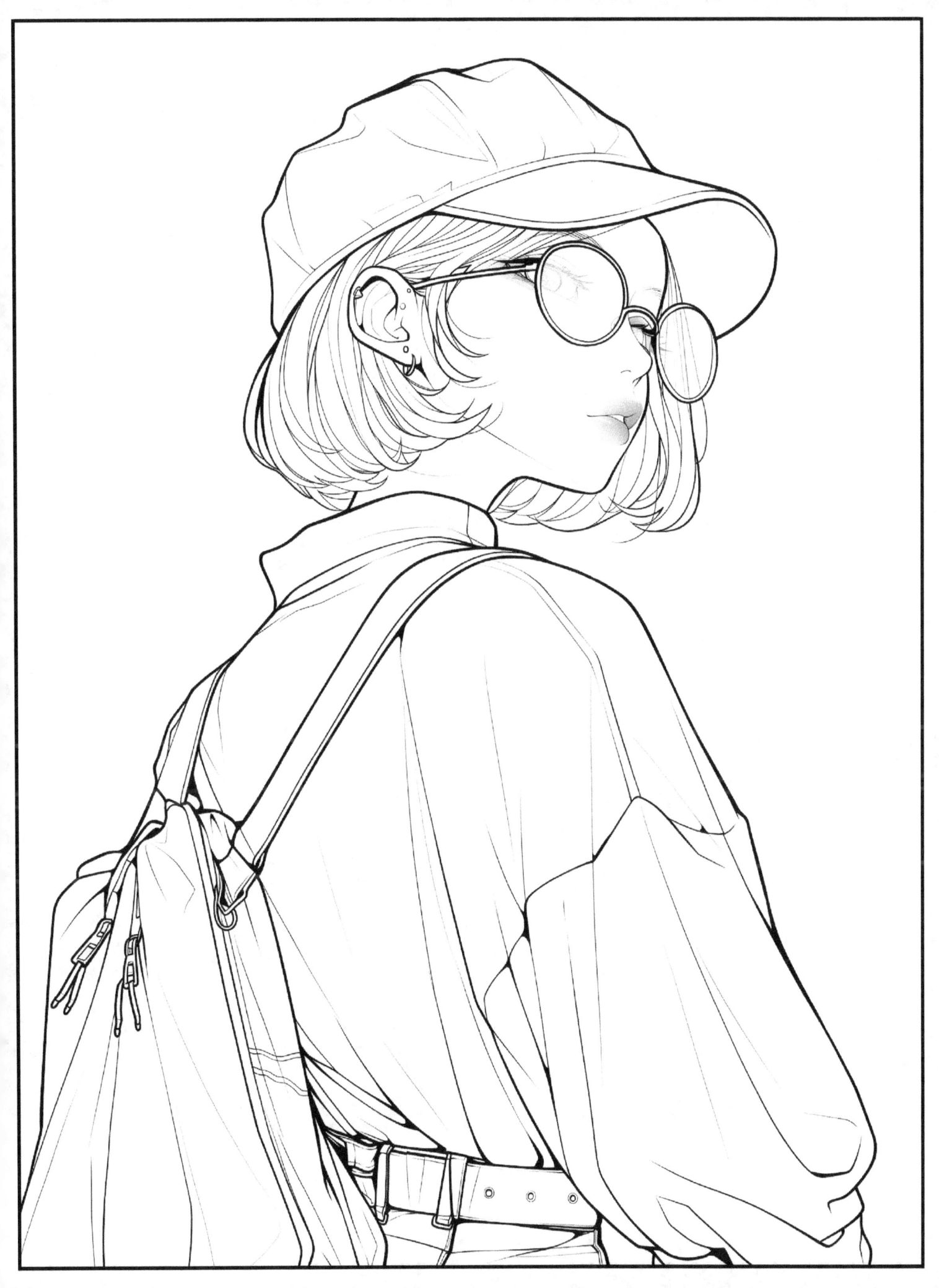

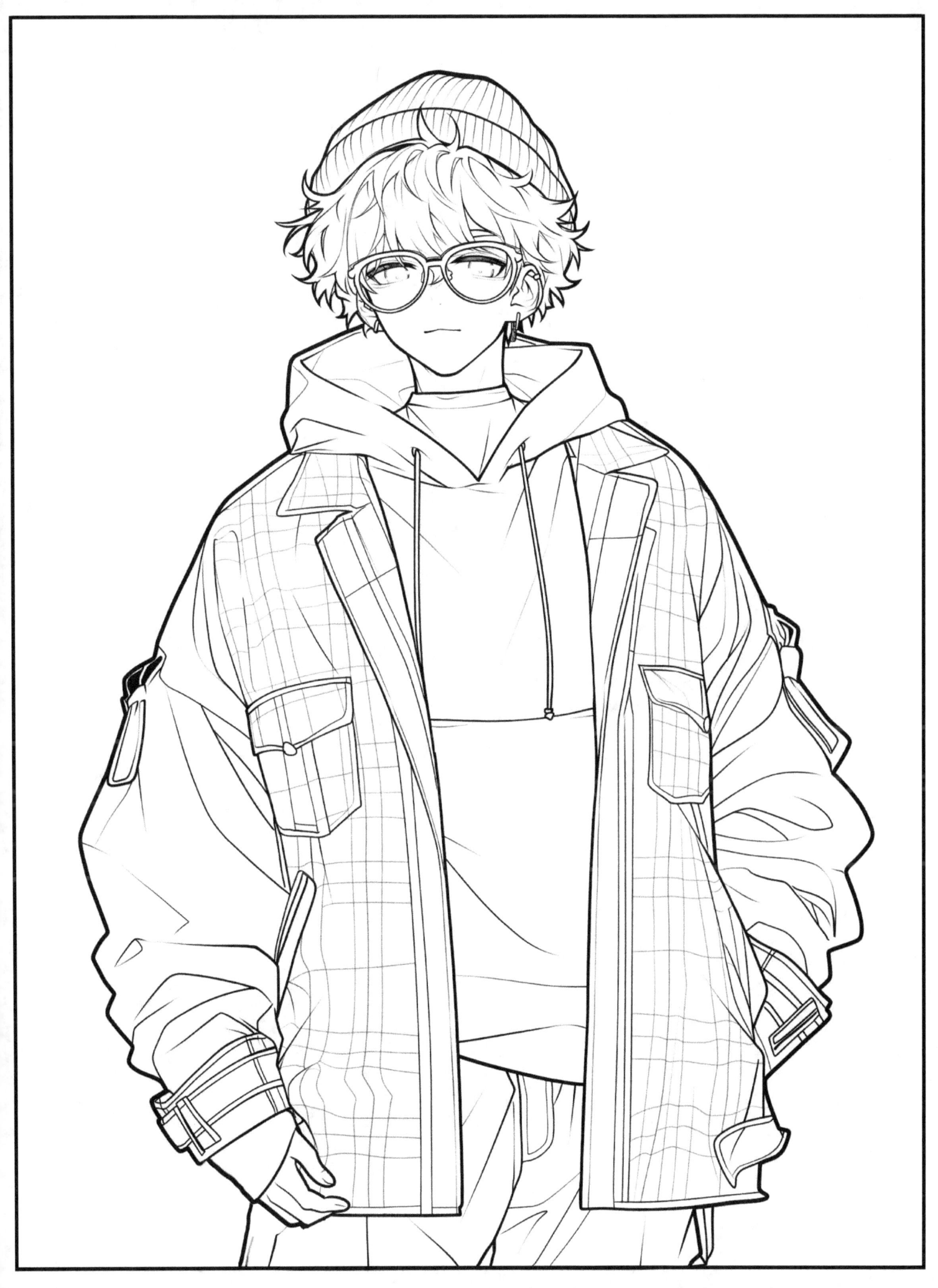

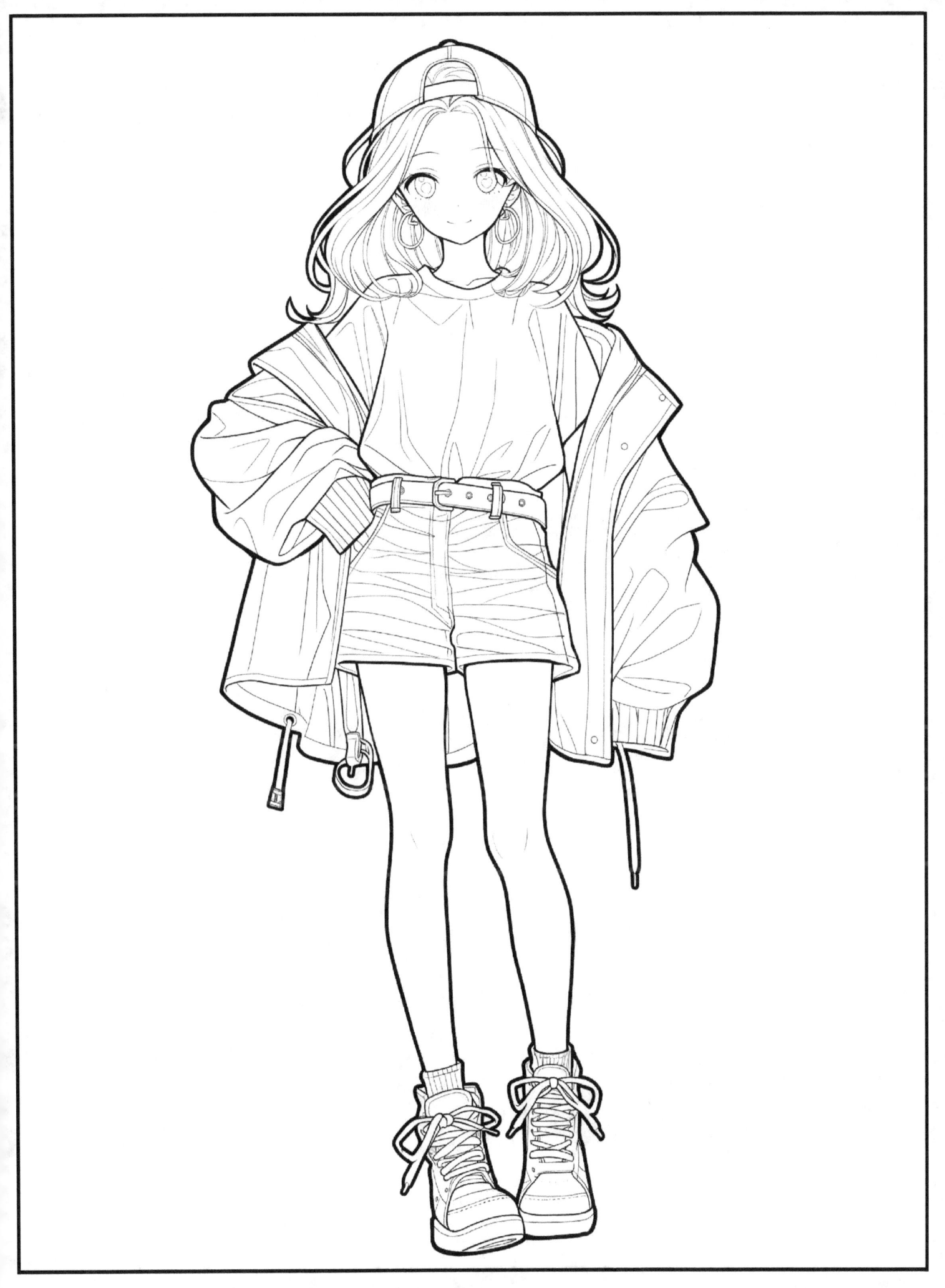

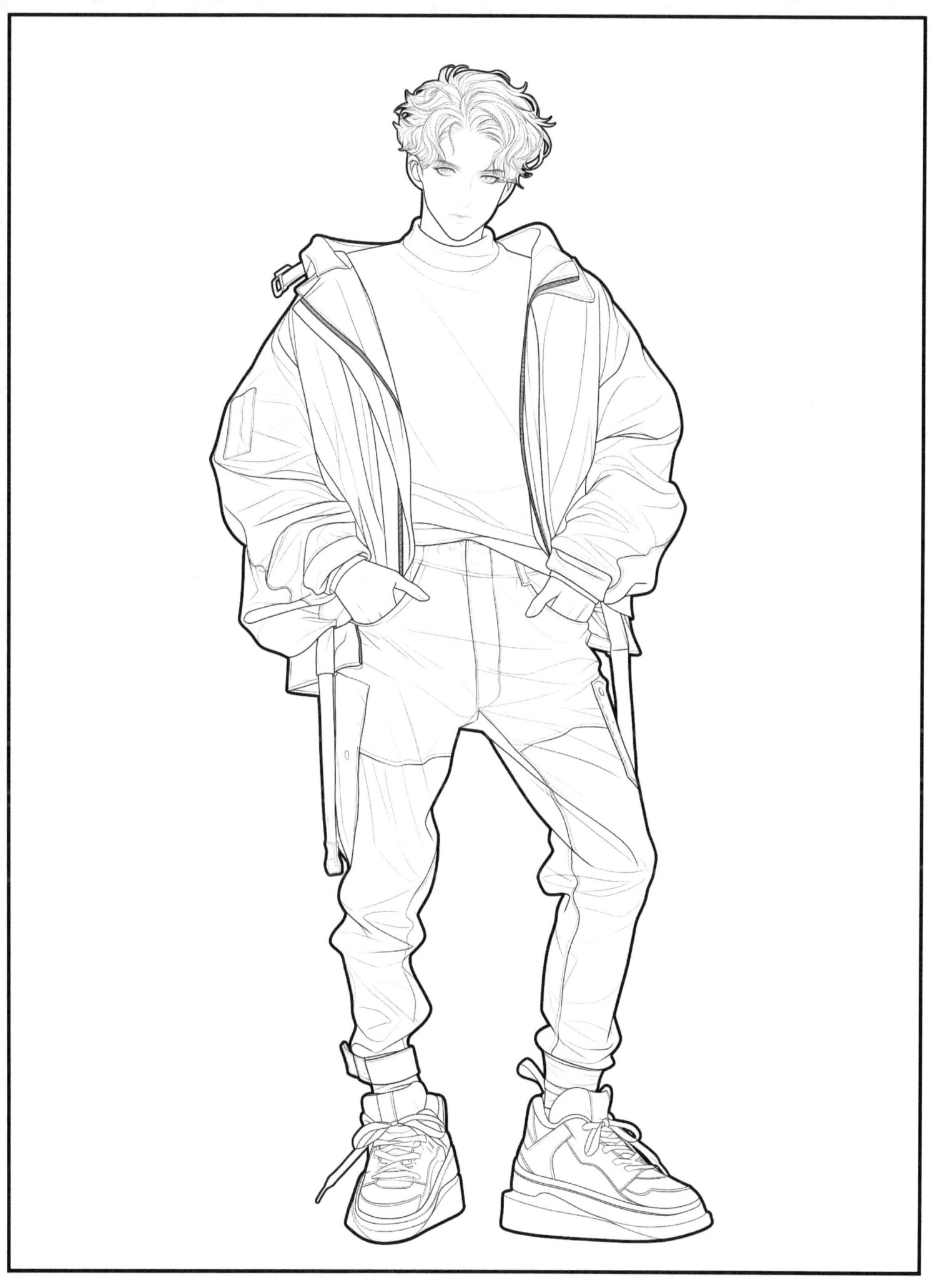

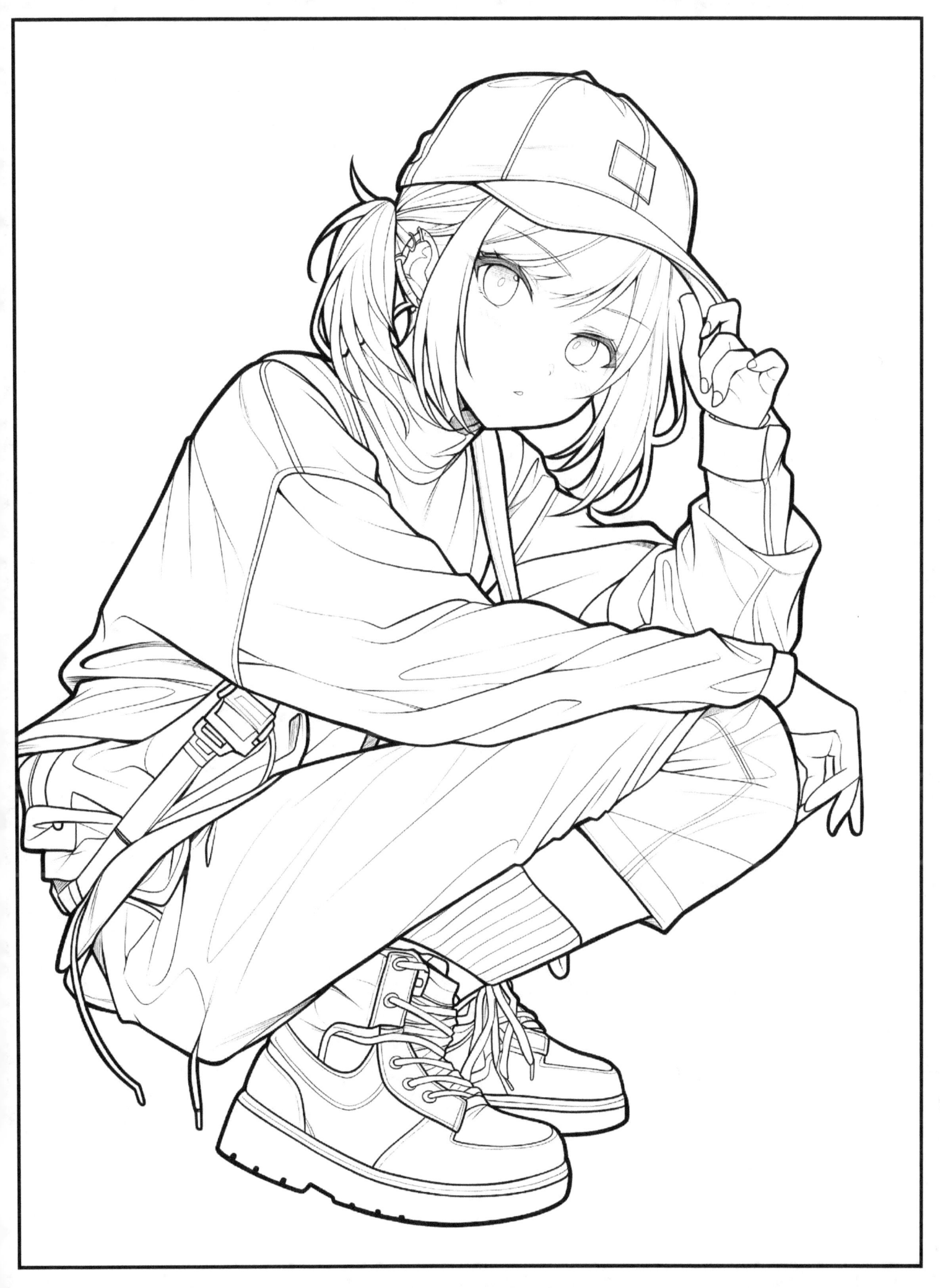

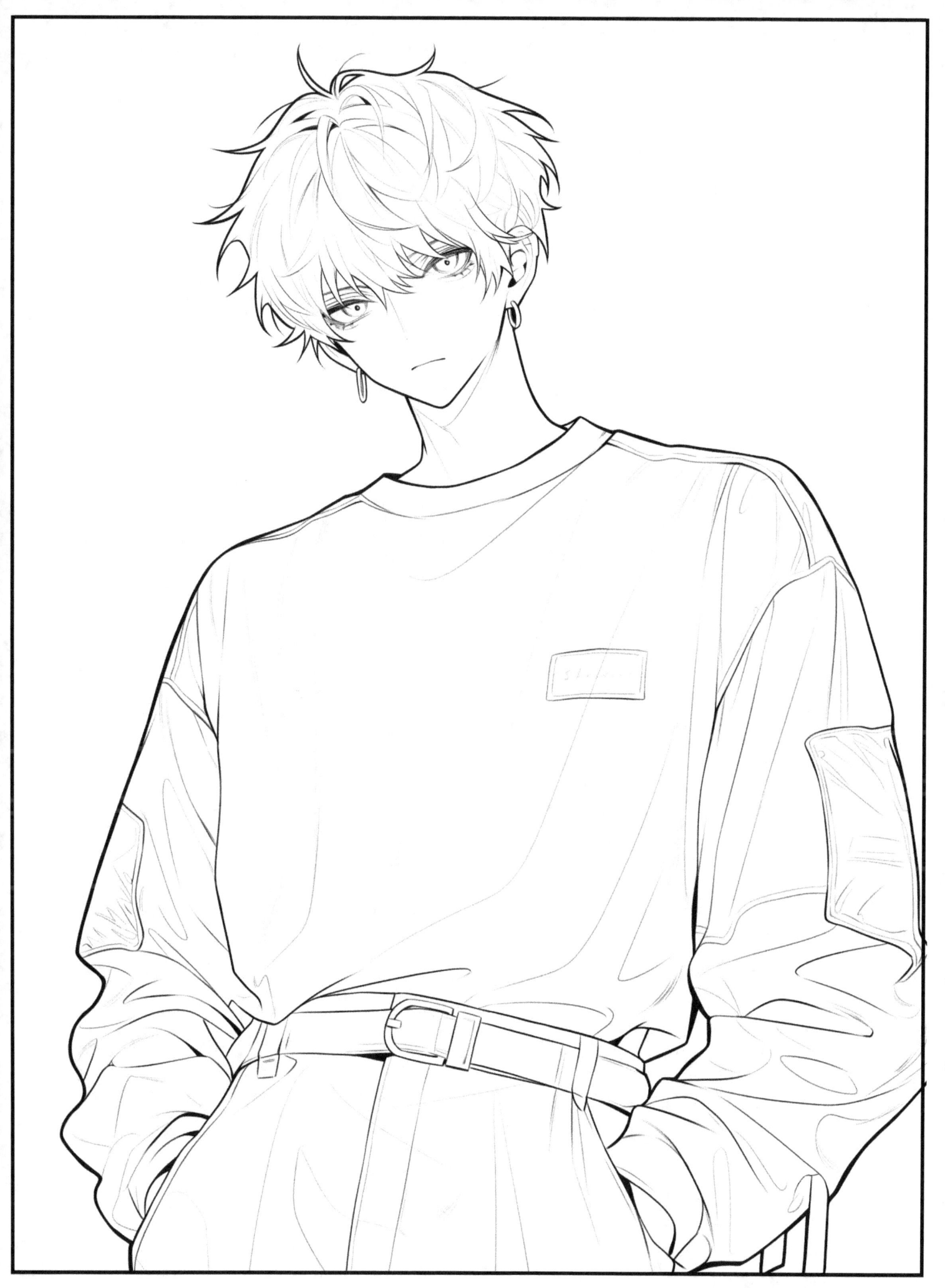

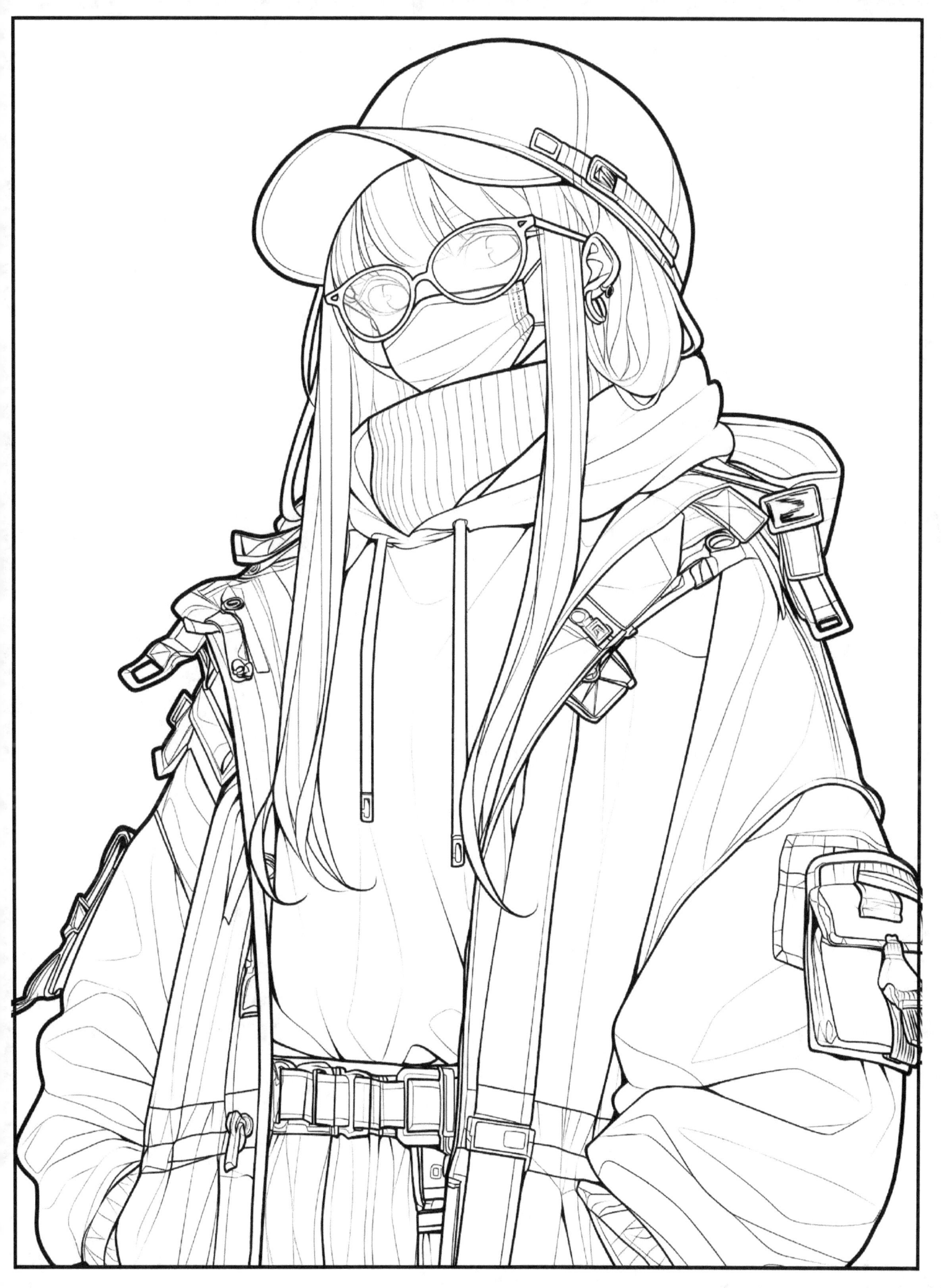

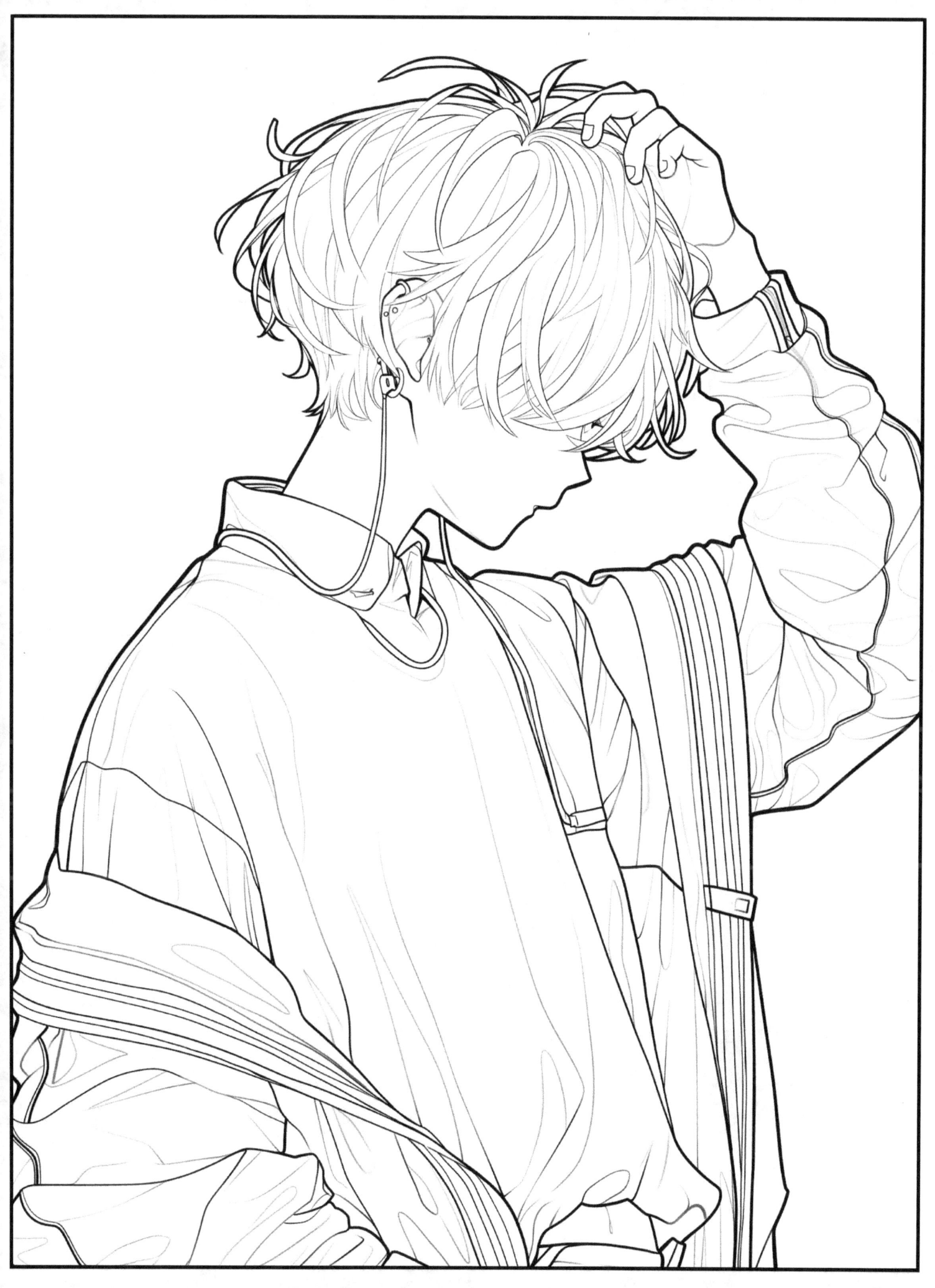

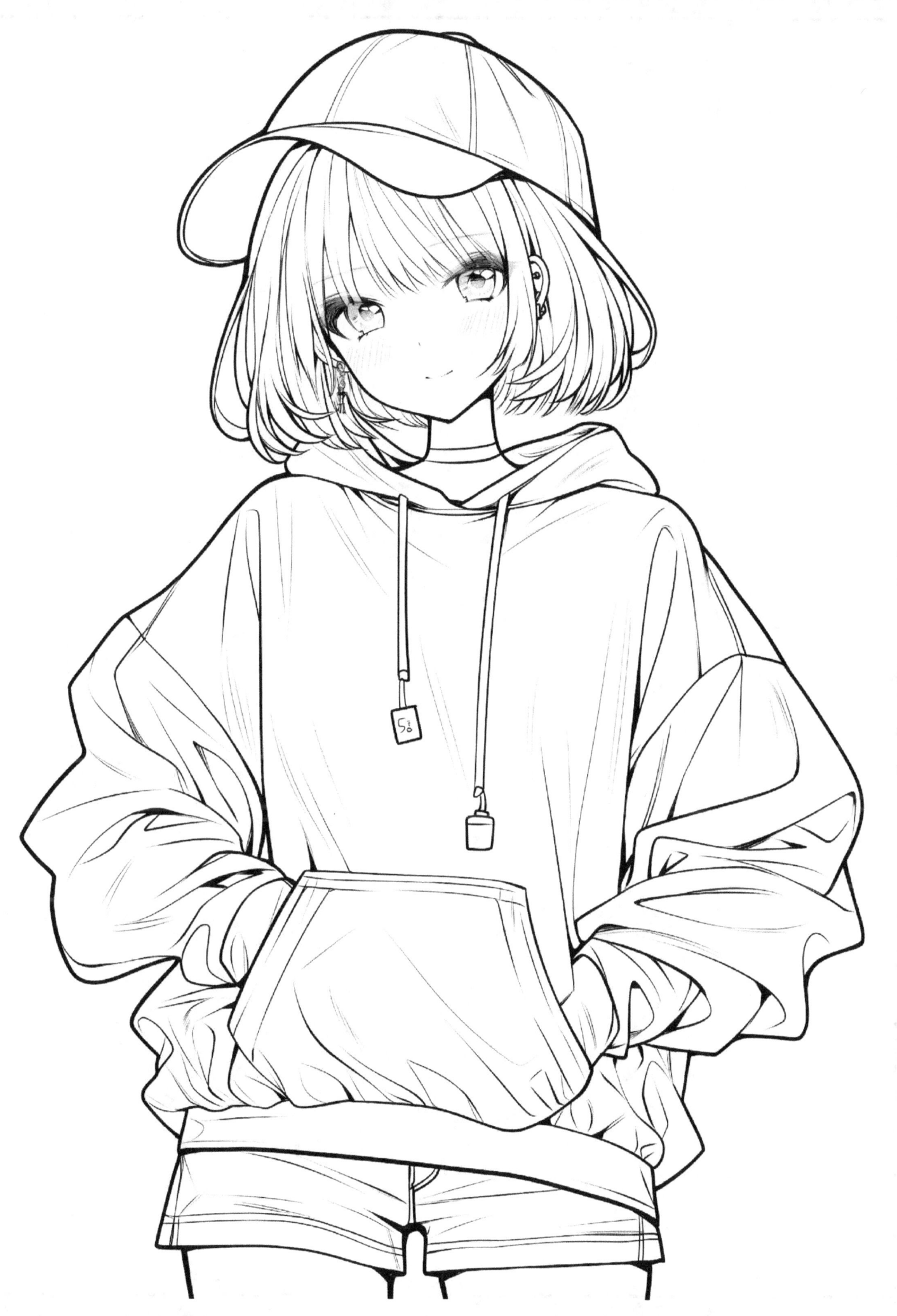

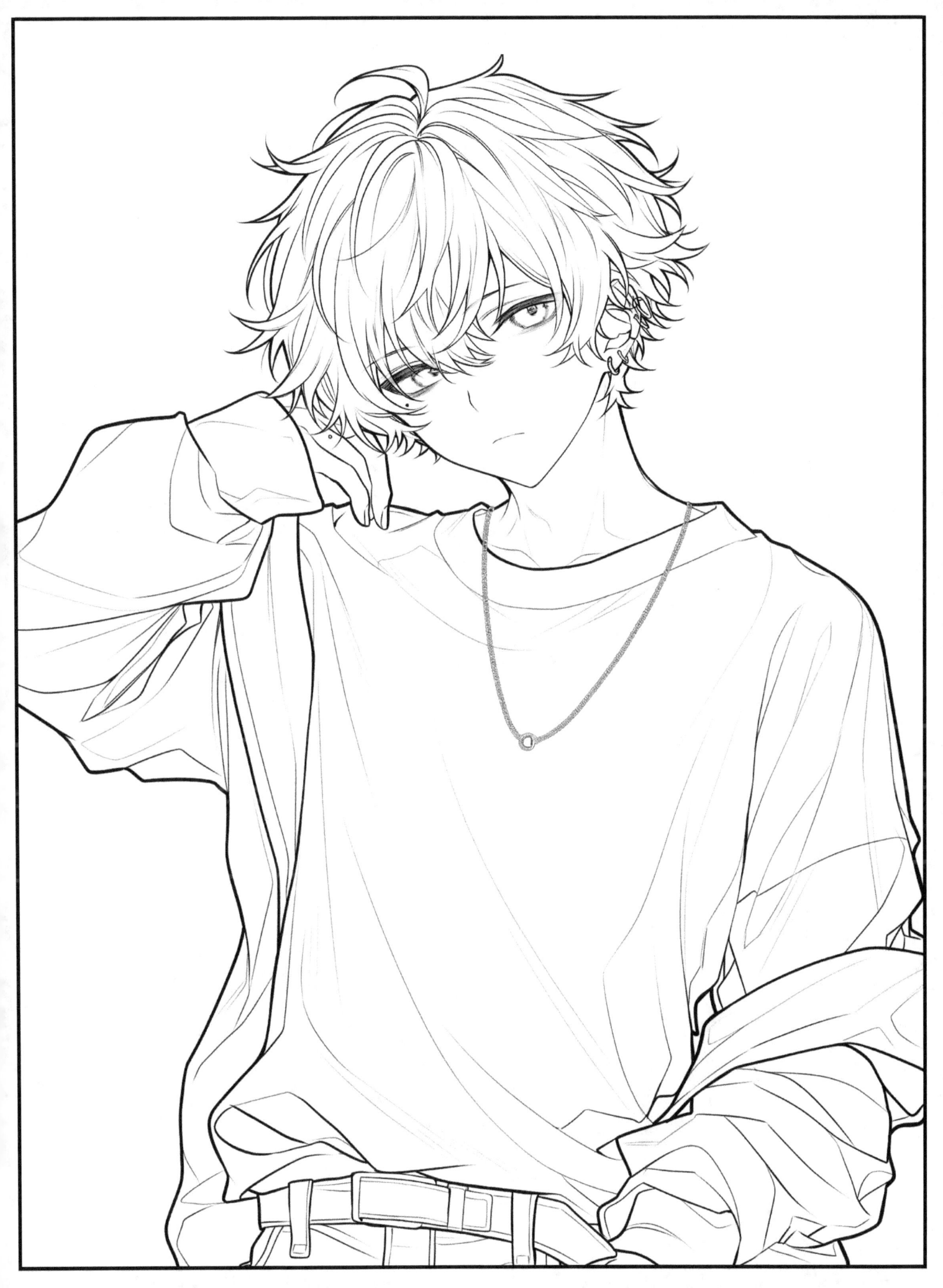

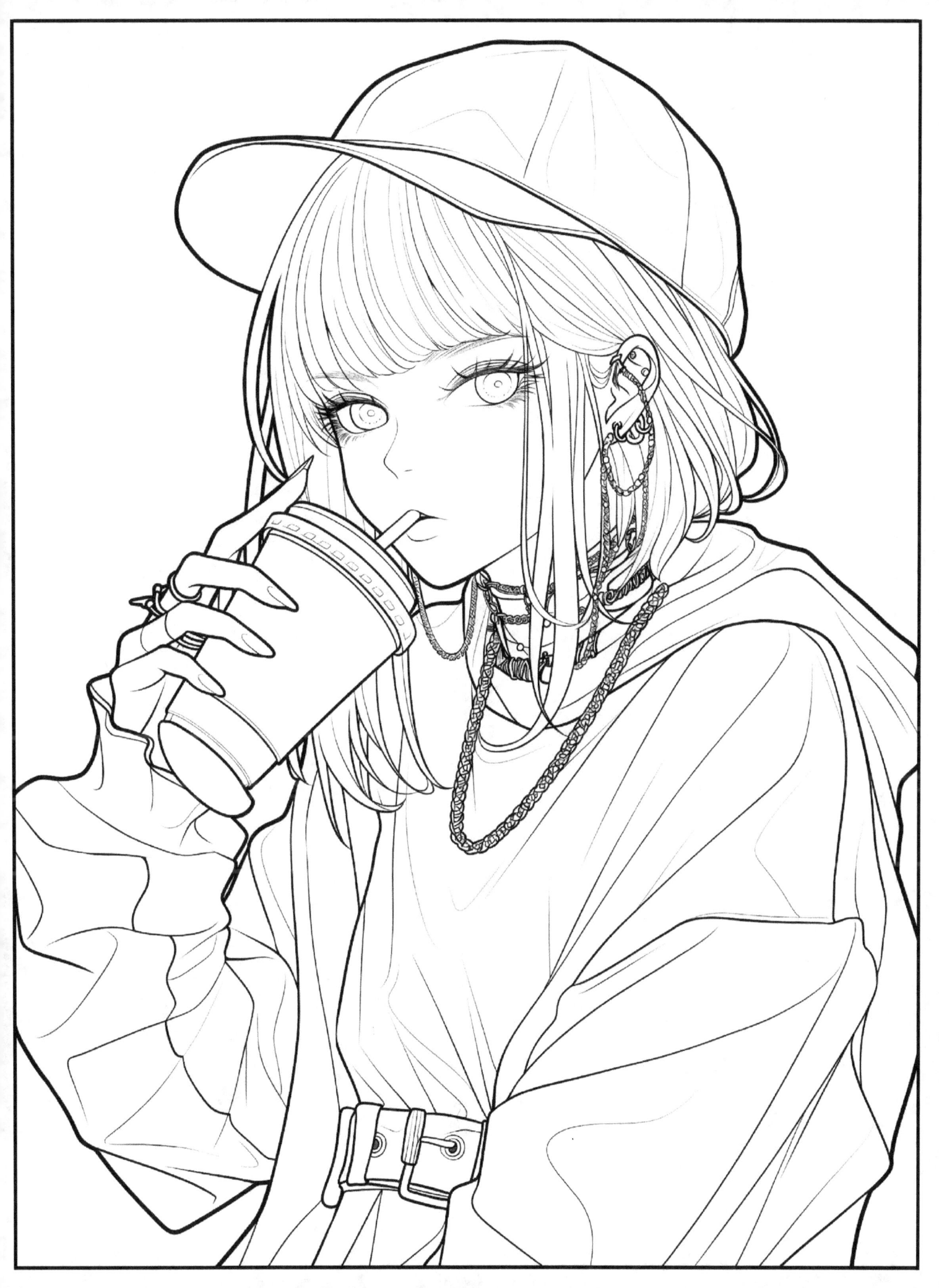

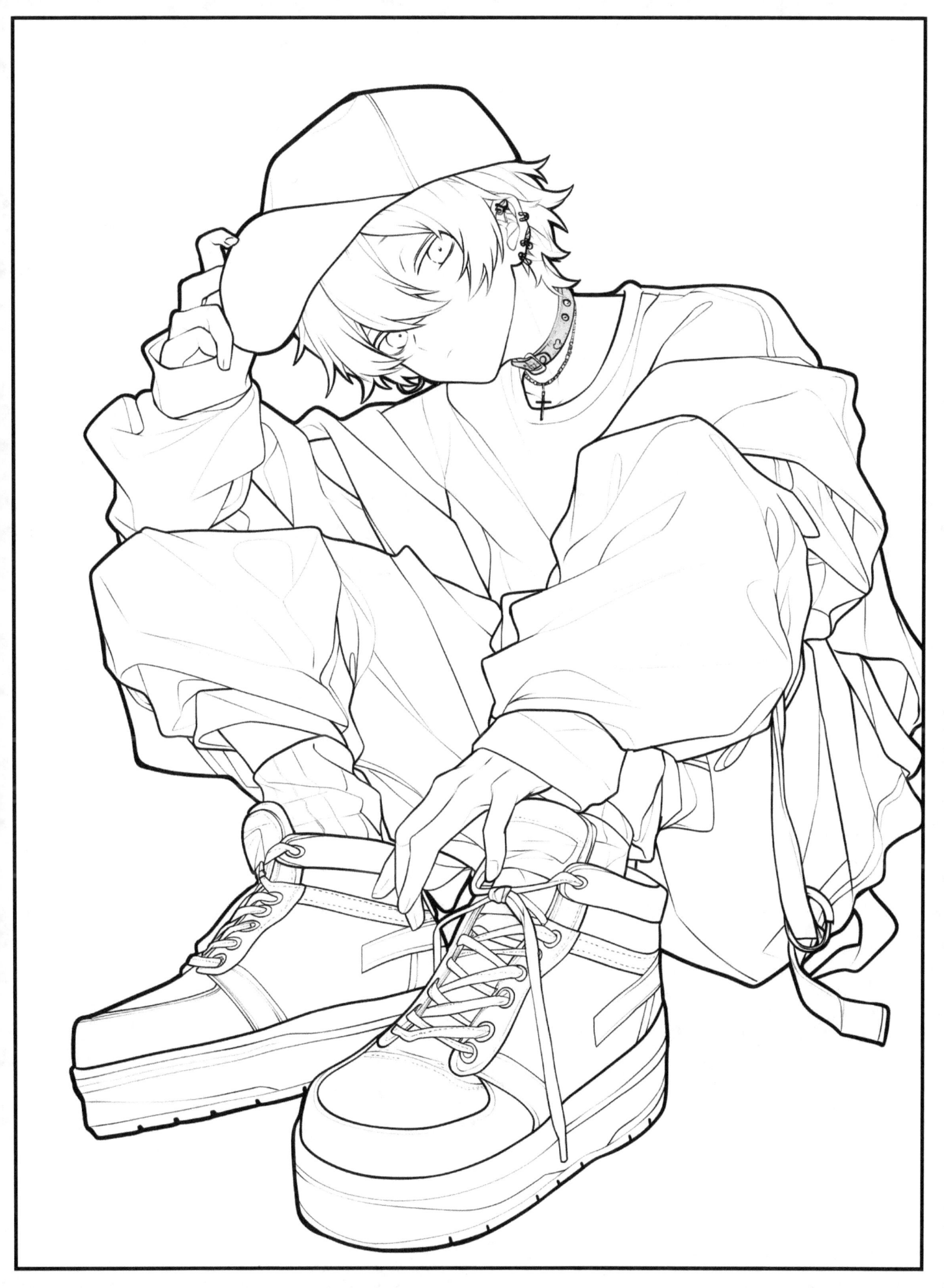

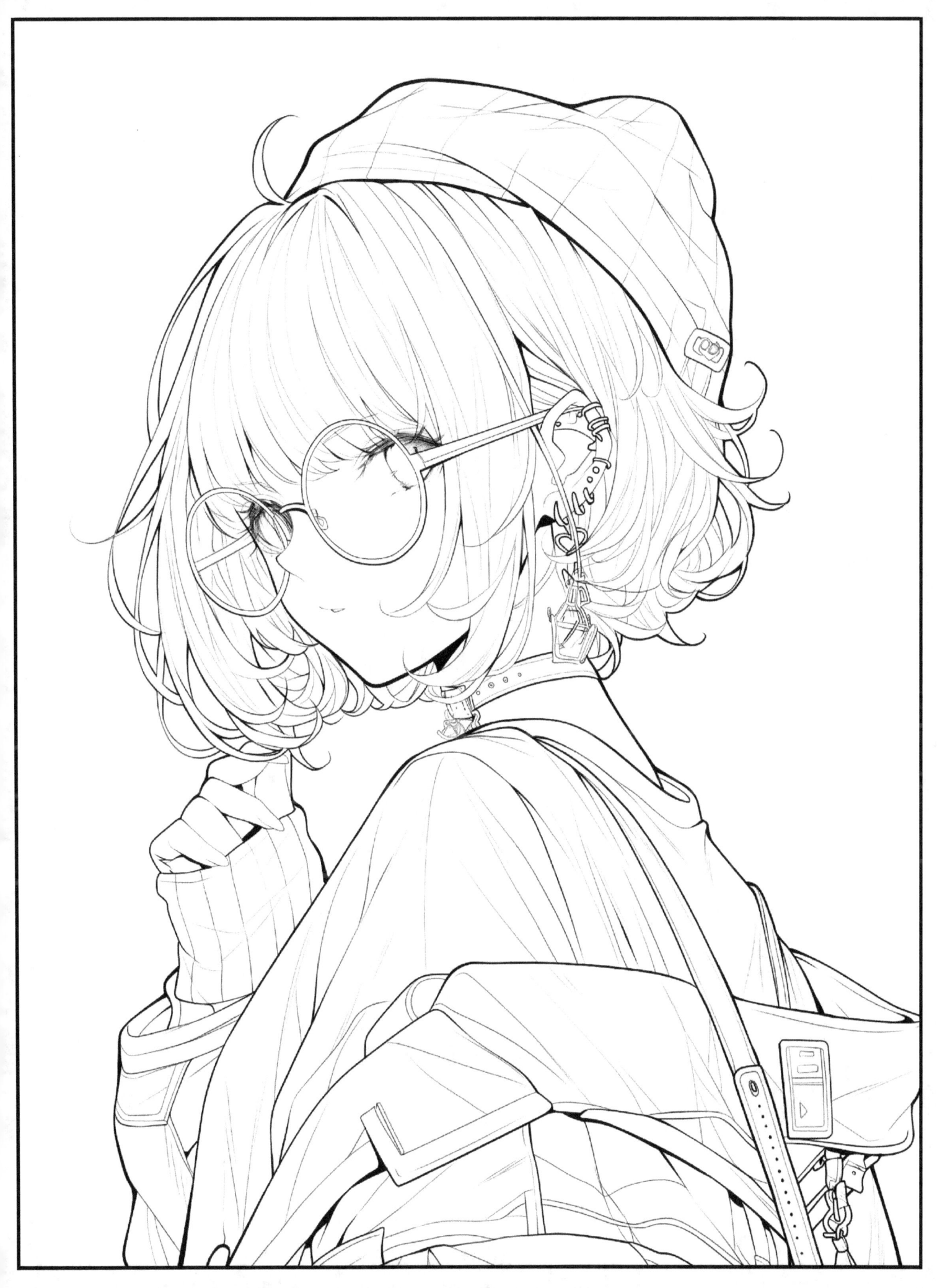

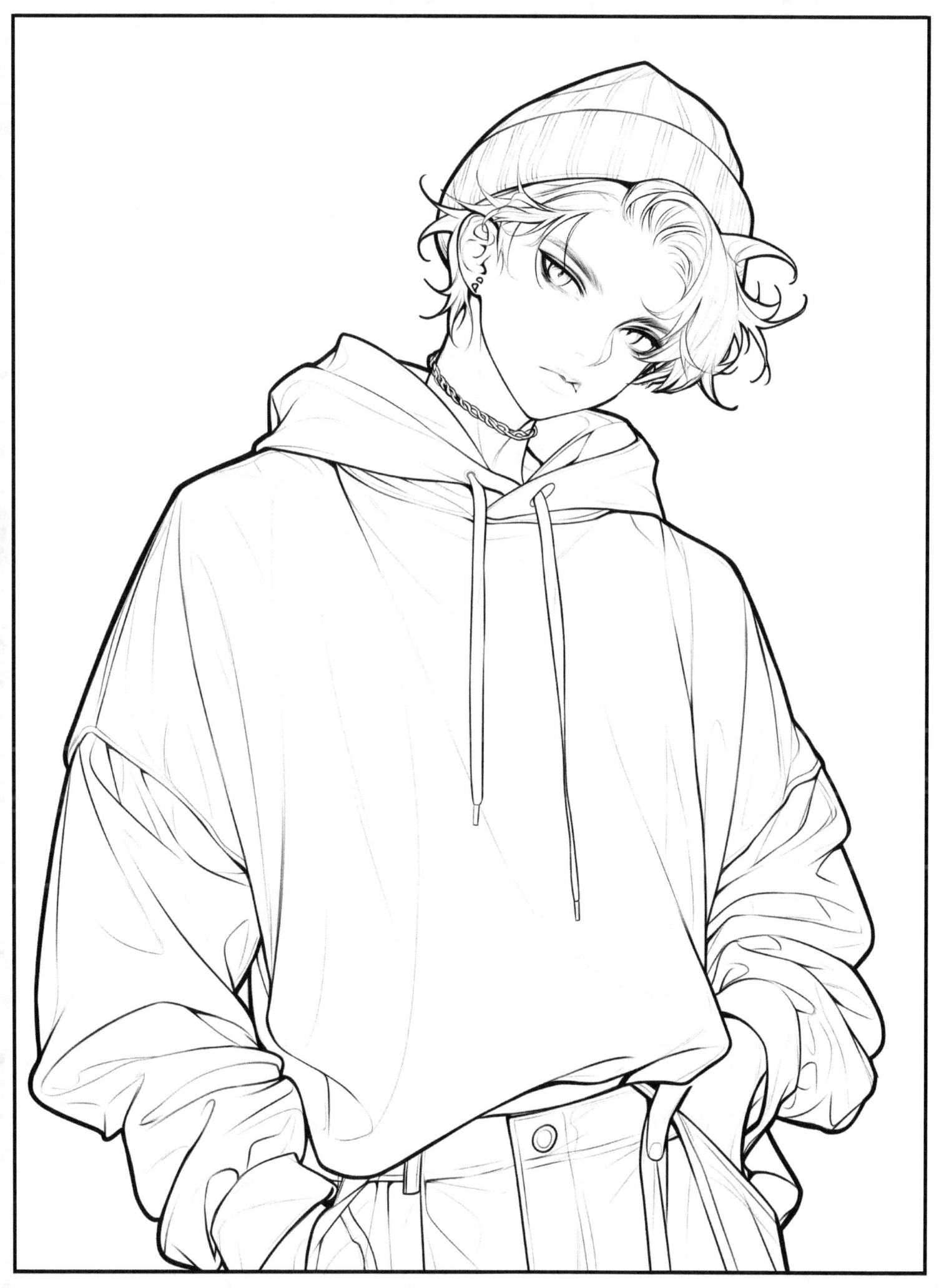

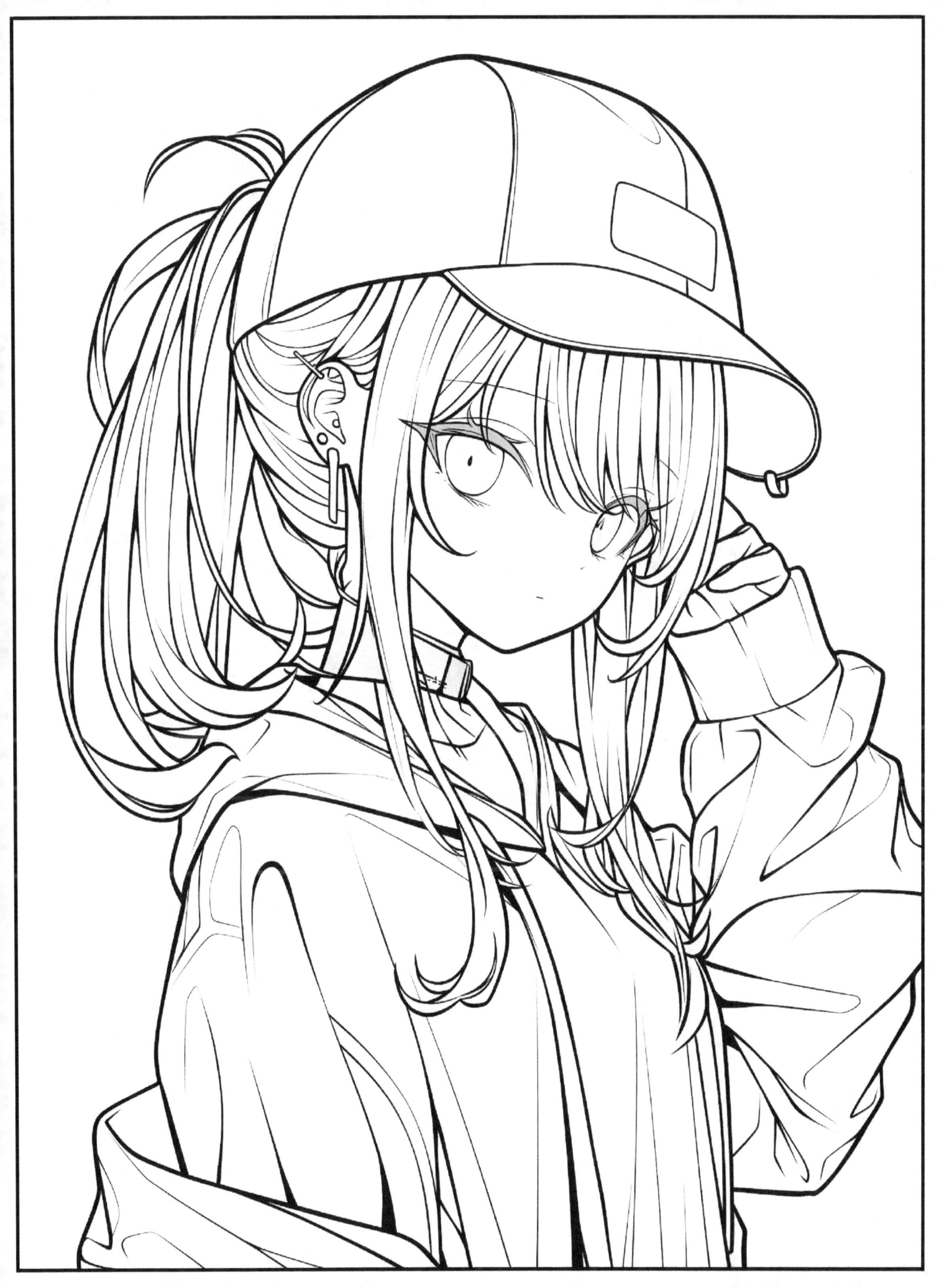

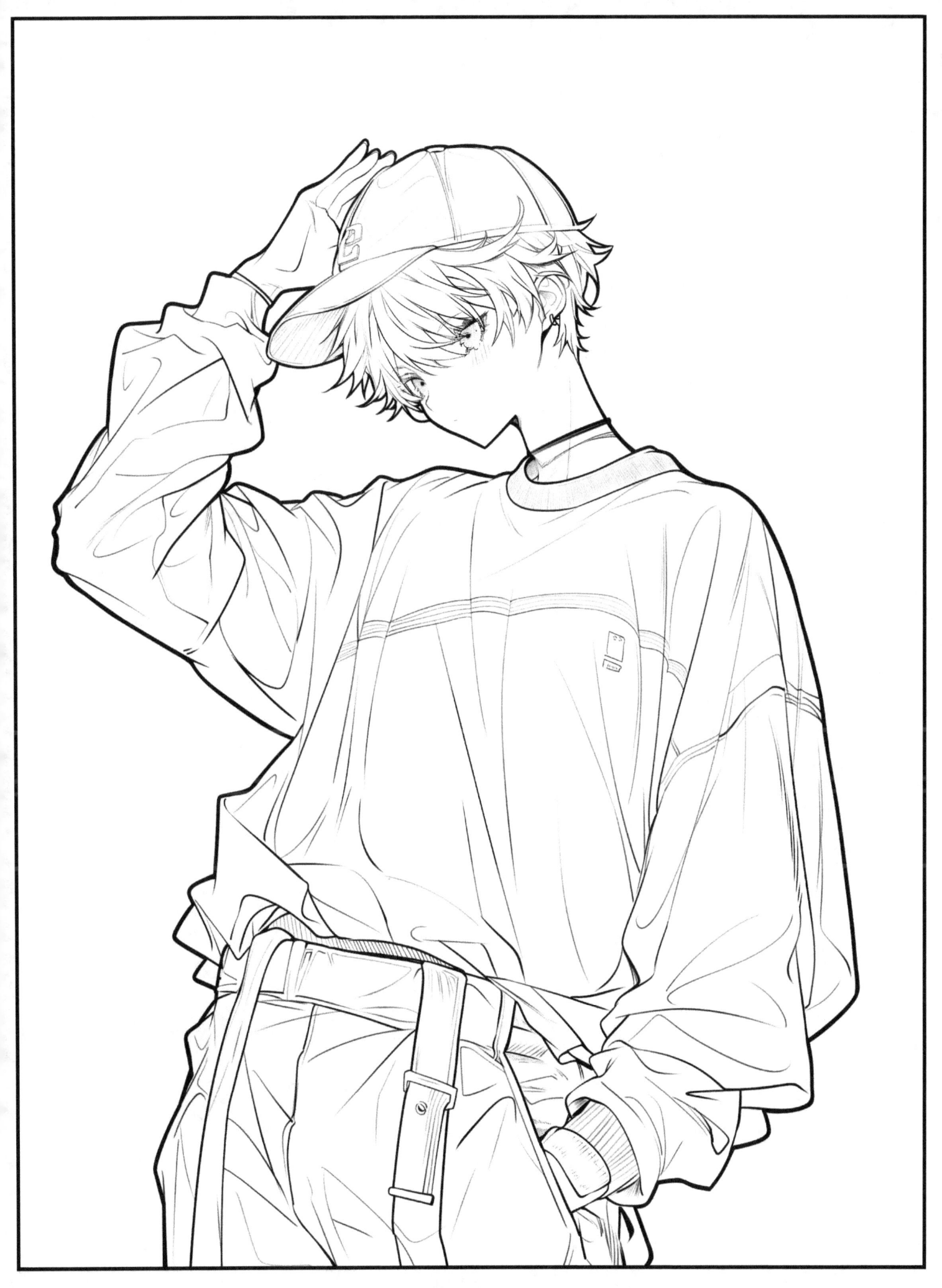

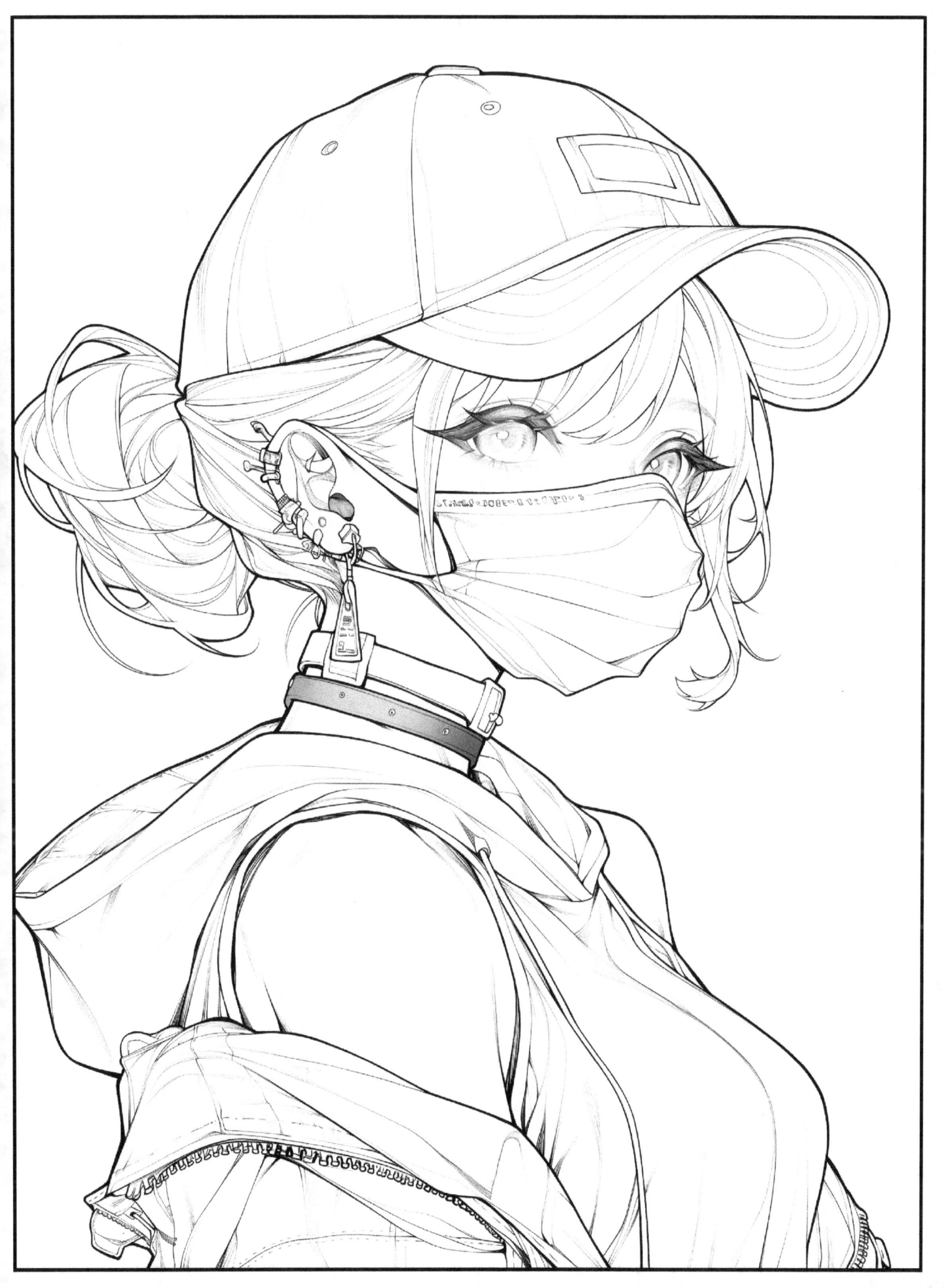

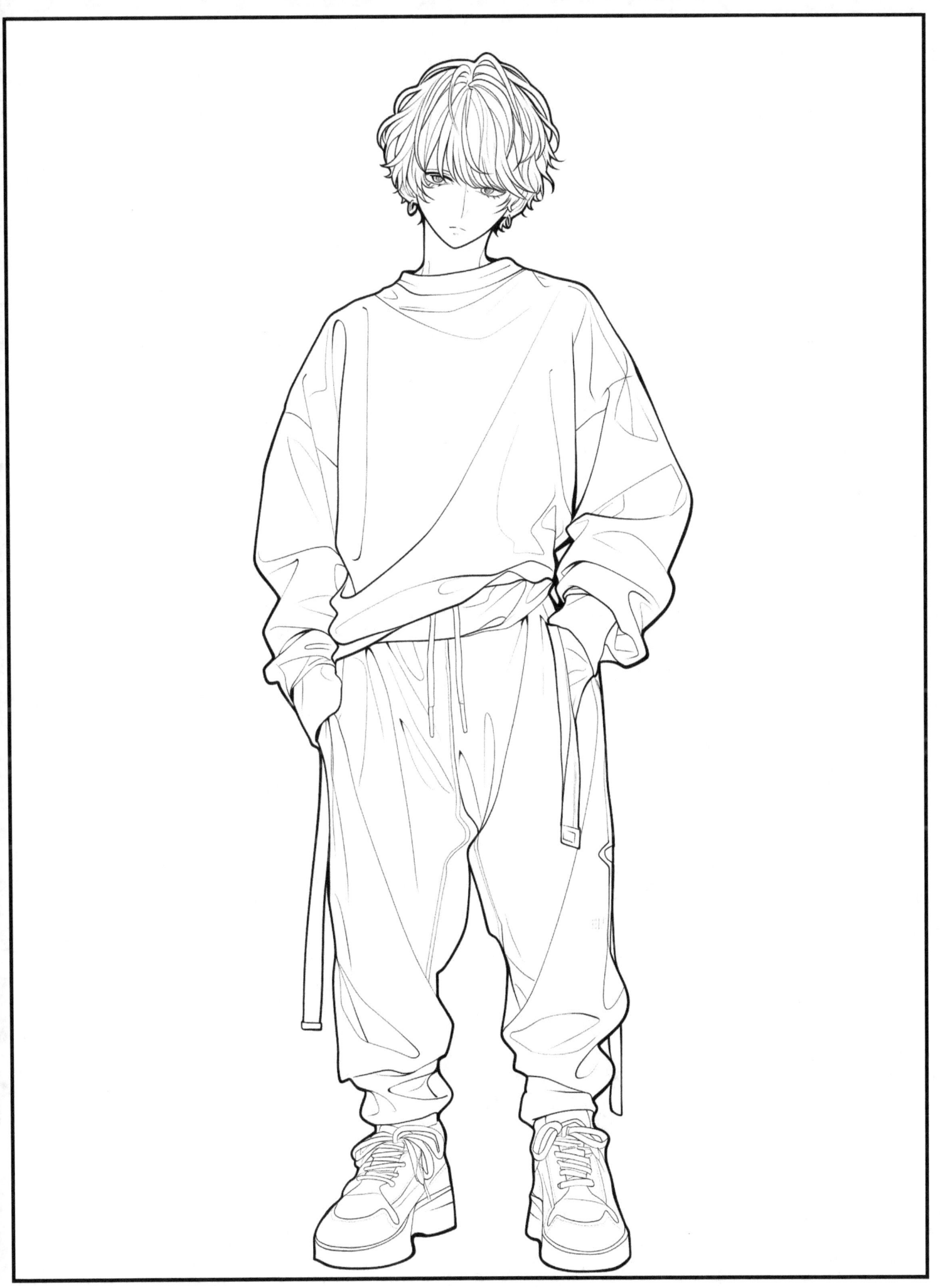

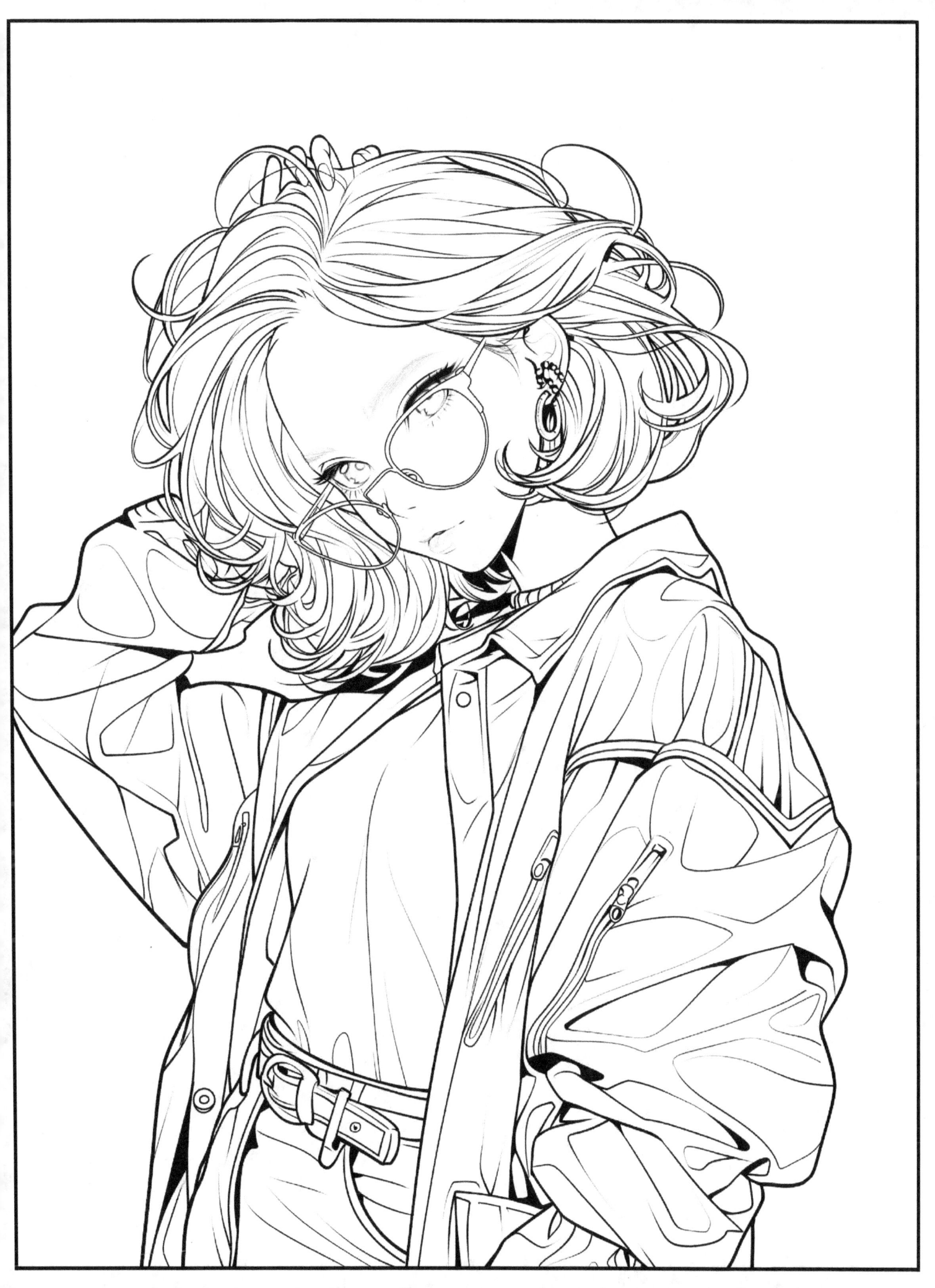

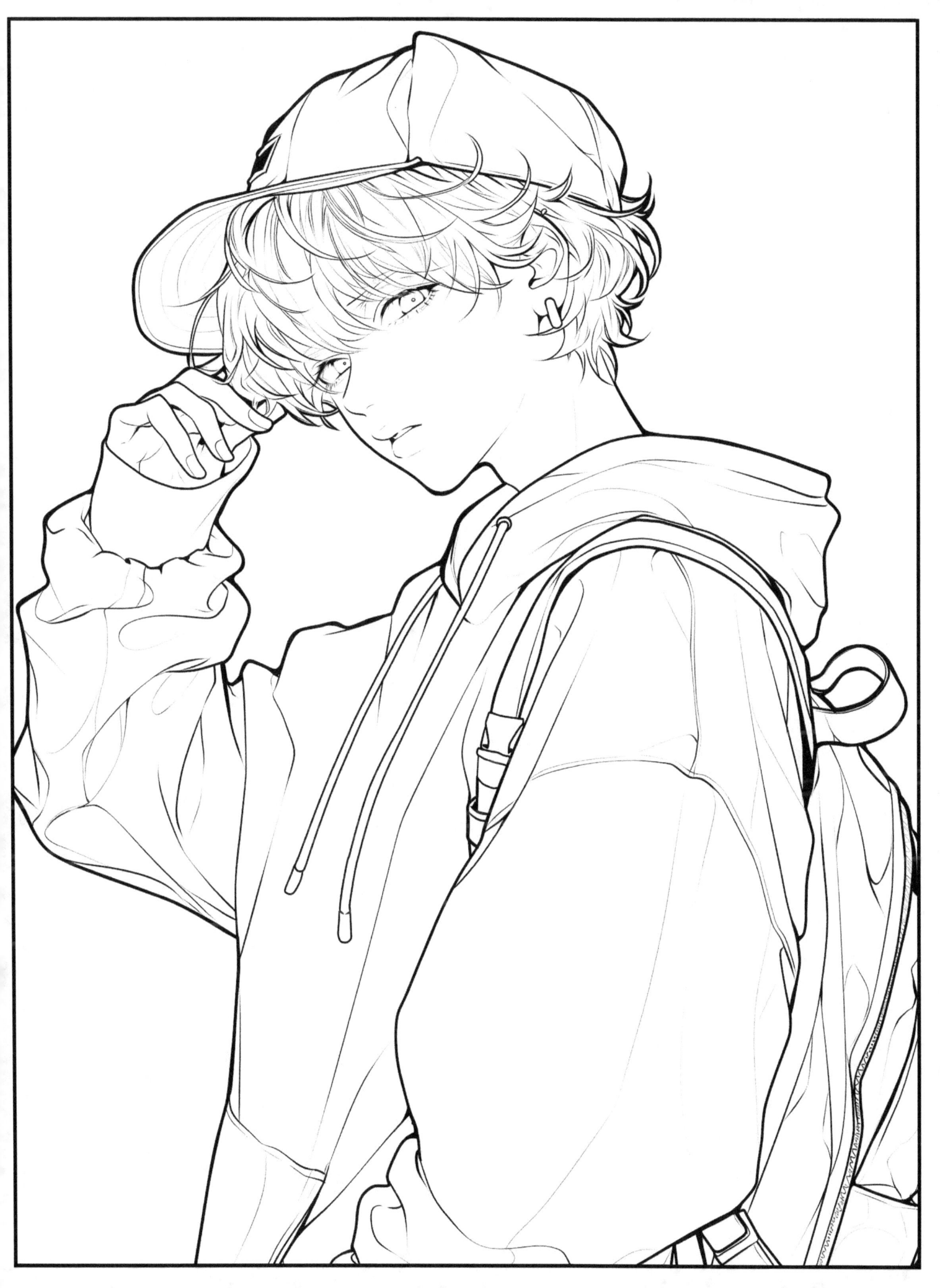

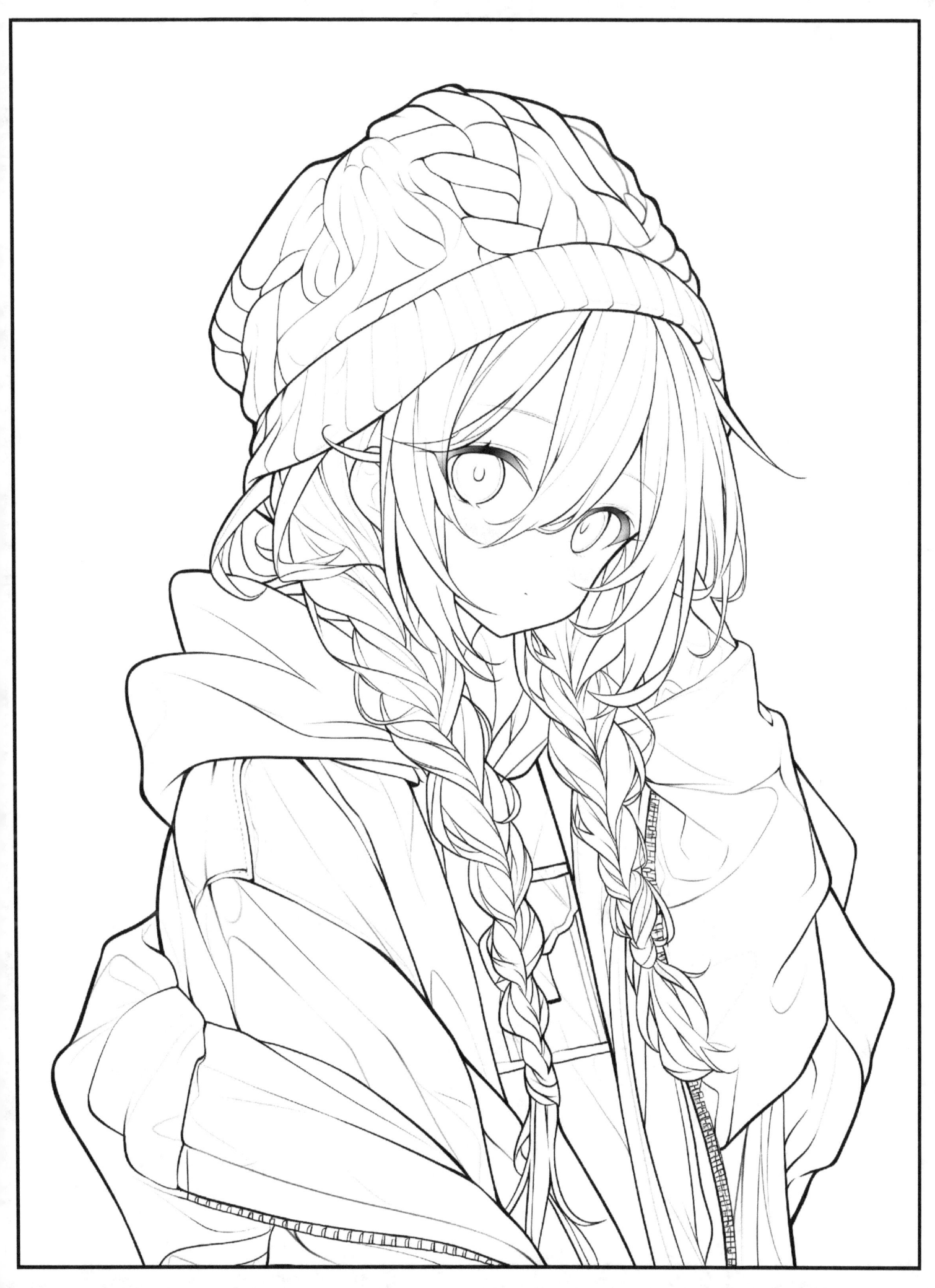

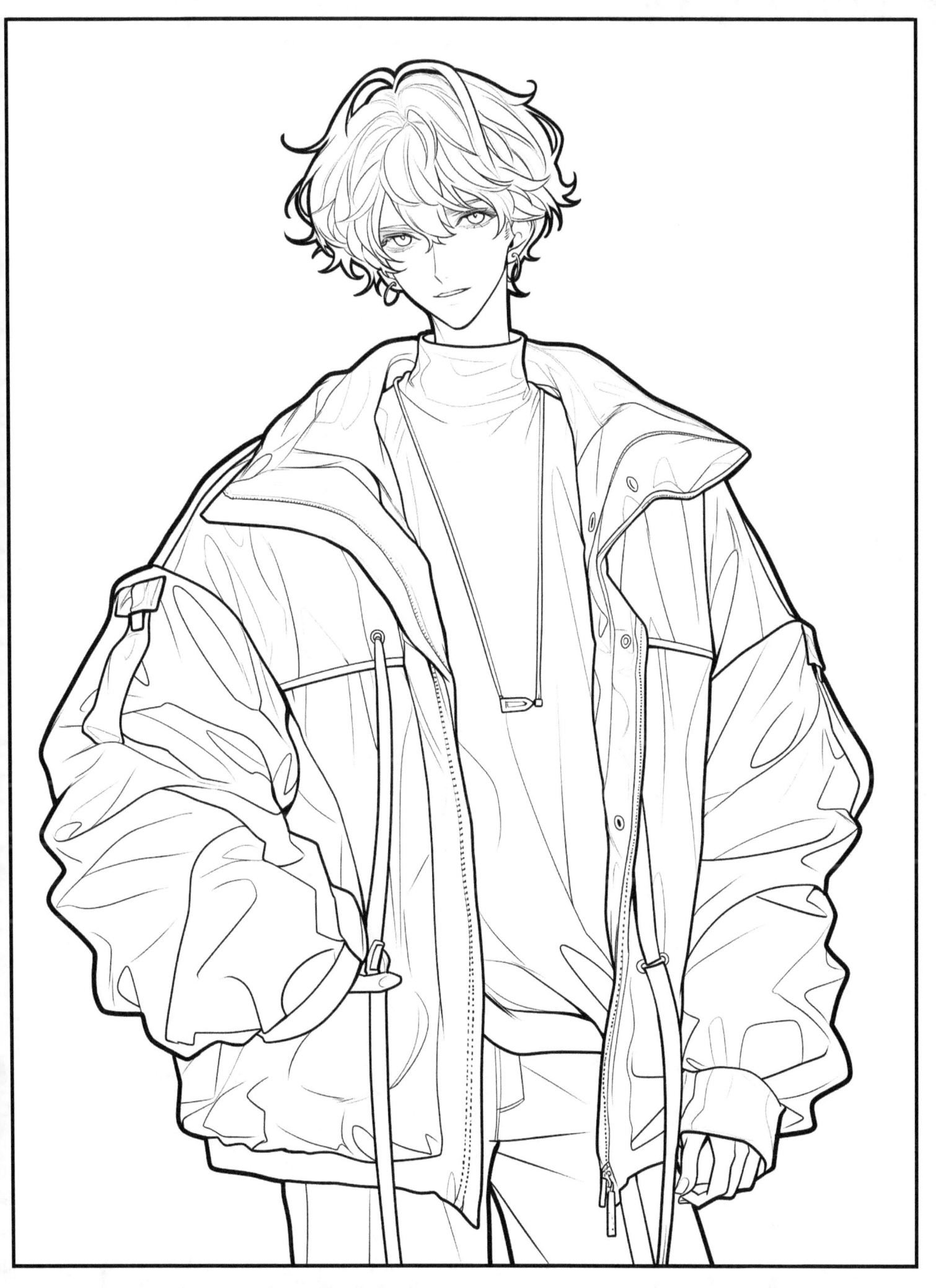

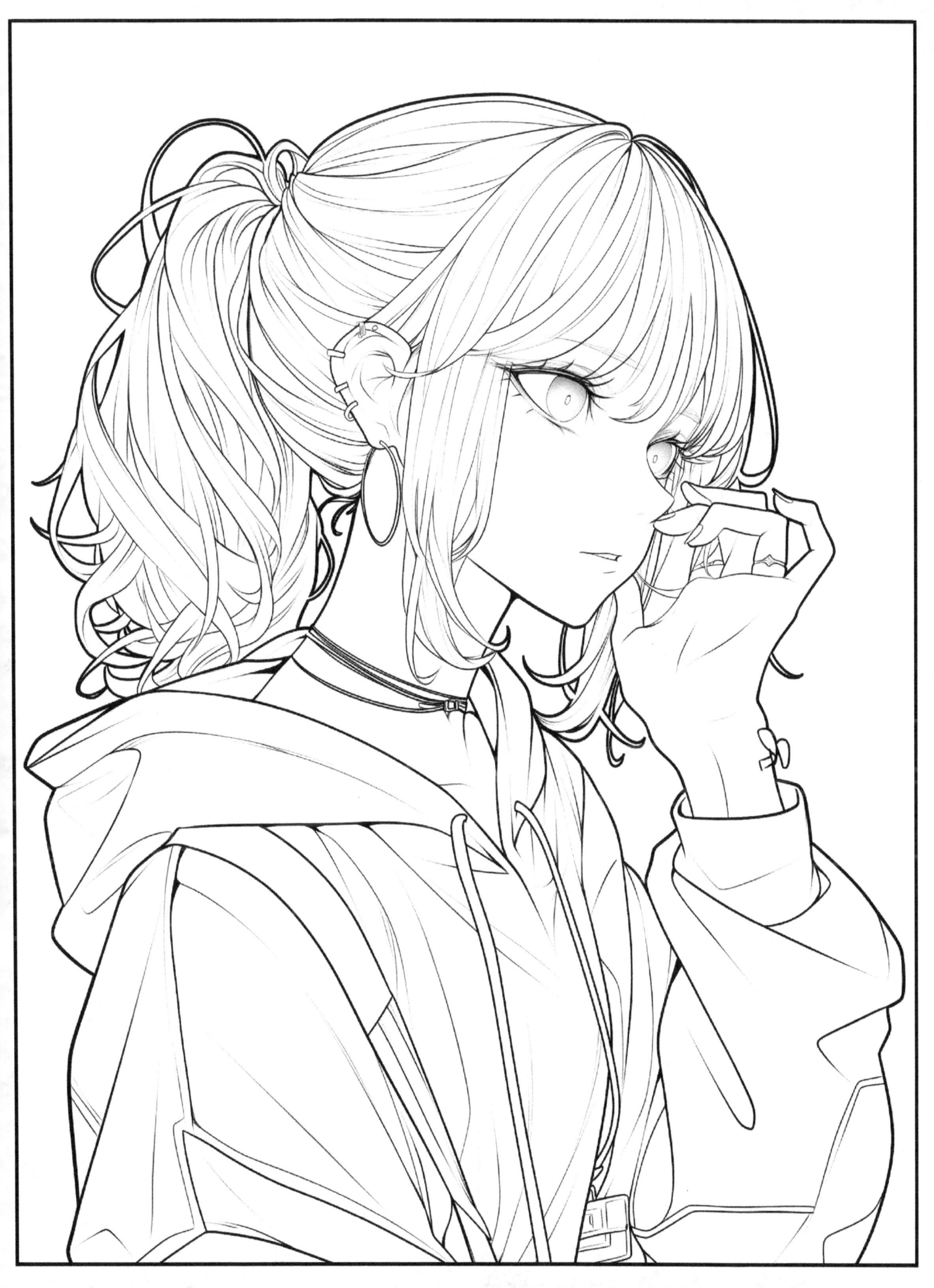

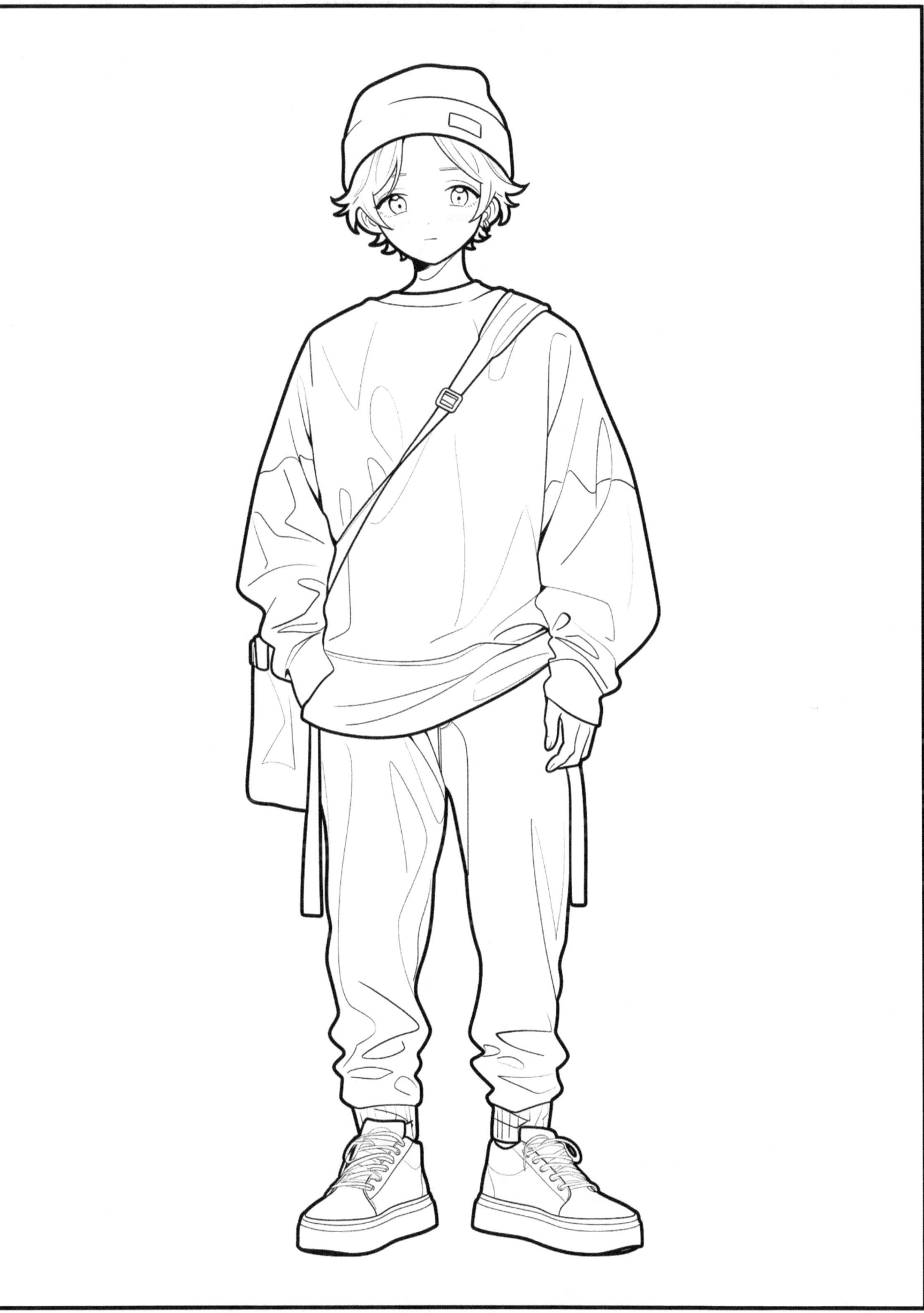

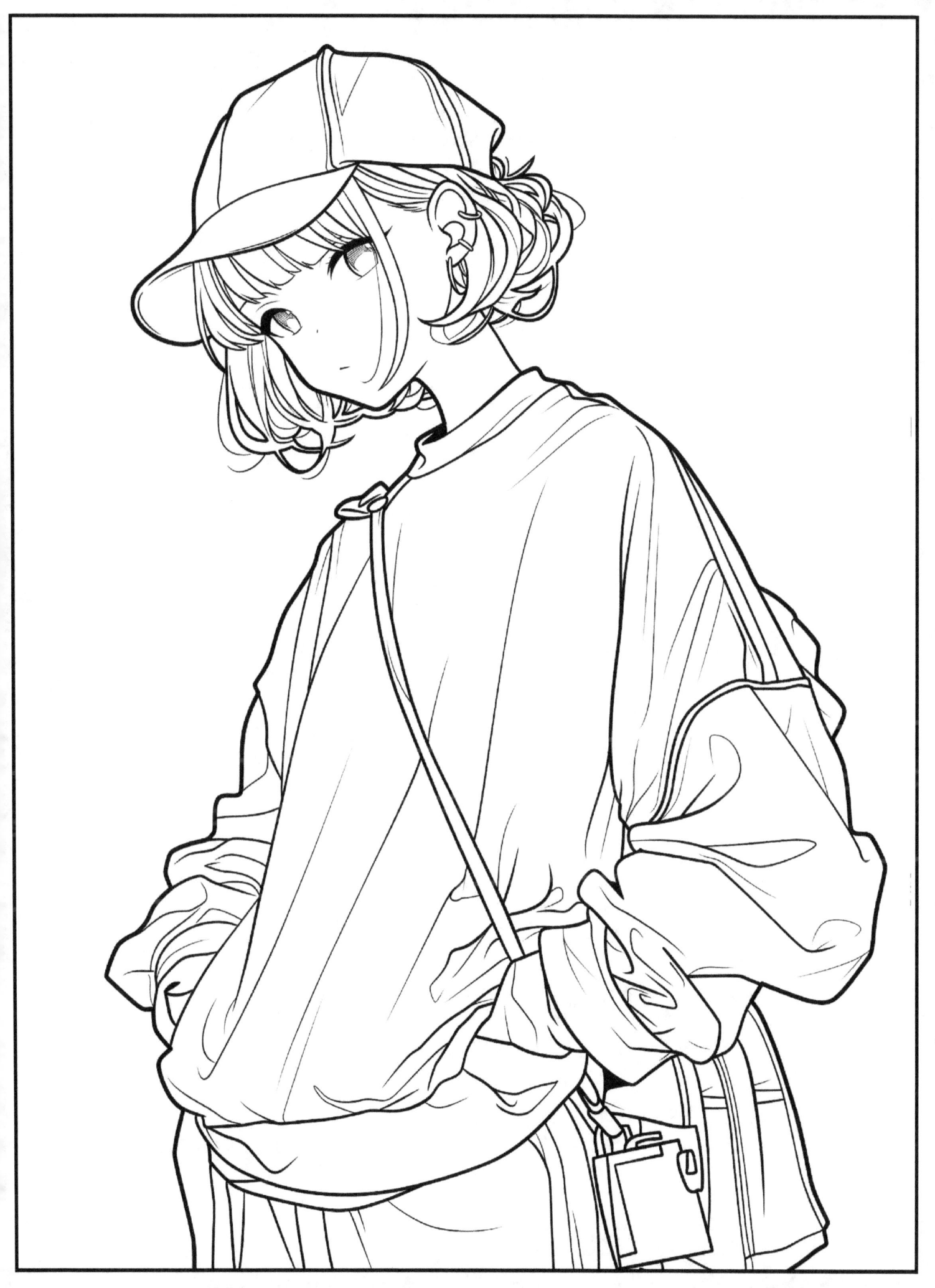

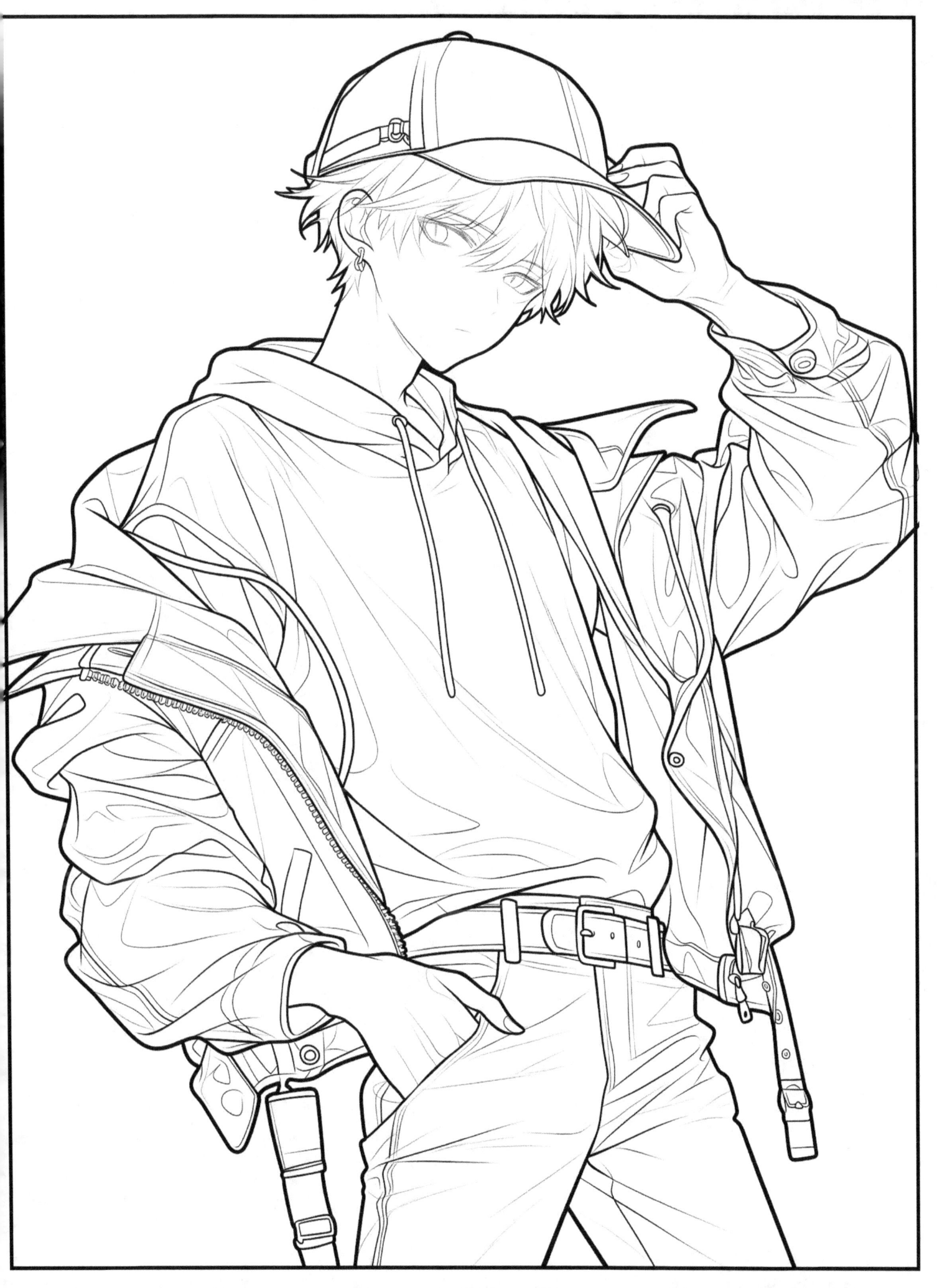

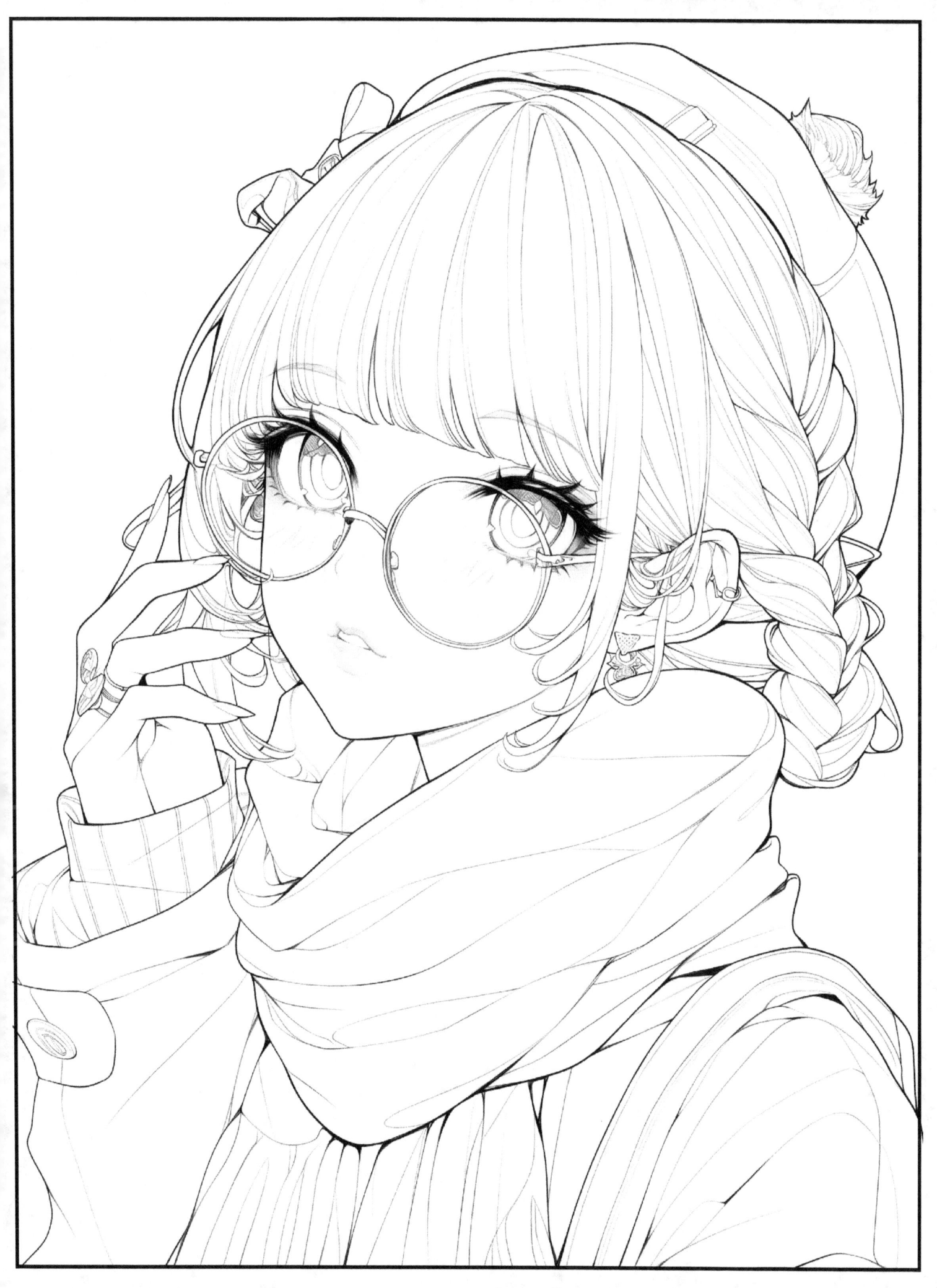

www.ingramcontent.com/pod-product-compliance
Lightning Source LLC
Chambersburg PA
CBHW080000230526
45470CB00008B/2810